ESCAPING THE SUBTLE SELLOUT

DEWEY BERTOLINI

KIRK FAULKNER
4200 NORTHEAST SAINT JOHNS ROAD
VANCOUVER, WA 98661

VICTOR BOOKS

A DIVISION OF SCRIPTURE PRESS PUBLICATIONS INC.
USA CANADA ENGLAND

Unless otherwise noted, Scripture quotations in this book are from the *Holy Bible, New International Version®*, copyright © 1973, 1978, 1984 by International Bible Society. Used by permission of Zondervan Publishing House. Quotations marked KJV are taken from the *Authorized (King James) Version*. Quotations marked TLB are taken from *The Living Bible*, © 1971, Tyndale House Publishers, Wheaton, IL 60189. Quotations marked NASB are from the *New American Standard Bible*, © the Lockman Foundation 1960, 1962, 1963, 1968, 1971, 1972, 1973, 1975, 1977.

Copyediting: Afton Rorvik
Cover Design: Scott Rattray
Cover Illustration: Grace DeVito

Library of Congress Cataloging-in-Publication Data
Bertolini, Dewey M.
    Escaping the subtle sellout / by Dewey Bertolini.
    p.   cm.
    Includes bibliographical references
    ISBN 0-89693-065-3
    1. Youth—Religious life. 2. Youth—Conduct of life.
    3. Bertolini, Dewey M. I. Title
    BV4531.2.B47 1992   92-12725
    248.8'3—dc20   CIP

---

1 2 3 4 5 6 7 8 9 10 Printing/Year 96 95 94 93 92

Other books by Dewey Bertolini:

Back to the Heart of Youth Work (Victor)
Sometimes I Really Hate You: Five Steps to Winning the Battle Over Bitterness in Your Life (Victor)

Written by Rebecca Bertolini:

Mom's Big Activity Book for Building Little Characters (Victor)

Contents

Two men have left an indelible imprint on my life:

Dwight Garland became a "father to the fatherless" when he took me under his wing and enabled me to transition from adolescence to adulthood. He saw potential in me when no one else did. The convictions that I have developed both in this book and in my life are the direct result of his influence. I will never forget him.

Hal Hale taught me to pray. I have known no one who walks with God more intimately. His simple, childlike faith continually inspires me to strive for the same. As a true spiritual father who has loved Christ for decades, Hal has passed on to me a spiritual heritage that I can never put into words, but one which I seek to live out in my life daily.

To both of these men I affectionately dedicate this book.

ACKNOWLEDGMENTS

I owe a debt of gratitude to Afton Rorvik, my *editor extraordinaire*, who patiently took my snarled strands of thought and wove them into a tapestry of color and definition. Afton, please accept my sincere and heartfelt thanks for a job well done.

To my students at The Master's College, whom I love more than they will ever know, thank you for tolerating my absence during the writing of this book.

And to my dear wife Rebecca, thank you for systematically building into the lives of our children the convictions discussed in the following pages. This book has been written with the prayer that David and Ashley will continue to strive to be two people of impeccable integrity.

Prologue

The scorching sun finally and mercifully began to dip behind the foothills surrounding my home. Sunsets in beautiful downtown Palmdale, California always signal a scurry of little feet throughout the house. "David, don't forget to brush your teeth." "Do you need to go potty, Ashley?"

As is their custom, David and Ashley came a-runnin' and, with pajamas flapping in their wake, brought their engines to full throttle and launched themselves off the middle of the living room floor. As they hit their target (my lap), the resulting concussion sent both me and my rocking chair into uncontrollable convulsions. Another day in the Bertolini household was about to come to an end.

With curtains opened wide, the majestic hues of flaming orange flooded our senses. Sunsets in Palmdale, I am convinced, cannot be matched anywhere. Soft music began to waft its way into the room, setting the atmosphere for our last few minutes together. As my wife Becky got comfortable on the couch, David wedged himself into the cavity formed by my left leg and the arm of my chair. Ashley popped her thumb into her mouth as she sat like a queen on her royal throne, proudly perched on my right thigh. *This is what it's all about,* I thought to myself. *Nothing can compare to these moments we share together night after night.*

But sometimes, in the midst of celebrating another sunset, I find myself a bit unsettled. I can hear my wife and children laughing and singing; yet at times, I feel strangely detached and withdrawn.

Like specters haunting the corridors of my mind, several images from earlier in the day shattered one of these tranquil moments with my family.

I remembered talking to Jennifer about her upcoming high school graduation. "Boy, I'll bet you're excited," I blared. Everyone in the room looked up at my momentary surge in volume. Jennifer said nothing. She just dropped her head. Finally, she muttered something. "What's that, Jennifer? I couldn't hear you."

"I said that I hope you can come." She paused, and then added, "No one else is coming to see me graduate. No one else really cares."

Mark keeps getting into trouble. "Incorrigible," his teachers describe him. "A hellion on wheels," adds his counselor.

"I don't know why," Mark moaned. "Things just set me off. I feel sometimes like a walking volcano ready to explode at anything or anyone who comes along."

"Have you ever talked to your dad about these feelings?" I asked.

"Yeah, right. Talk to my dad? Which one?"

Somehow Bob and I started talking about relationships. "I've slept with just about every girl I've gone out with," he declared with almost a hint of pride in his voice. Maybe he wanted to test me, to see if I'd go off on some tirade about sexual purity.

I didn't. I simply and innocently asked, "Aren't you afraid you might get a girl pregnant?"

"Listen, my mom's been divorced and remarried so

many times that I've lost count. Now she's living with some jerk. I don't know of one relationship that has lasted longer than two years. You just don't understand. Every relationship I get myself into falls apart within a few months. I've got to get out of it everything I can while I can. Get a girl pregnant? Who cares?

"Yeah, I got a girl pregnant once," Bob continued. "No big deal. She just got an abortion."

"Do your parents know?"

"No way! They'd kill me."

He proceeded to tell me about his current girlfriend. "Dana's awesome, just the kind of gal I've always wanted. We might even get married next year!"

A few more minutes into the conversation I asked, "Bob, if you could wave a magic wand over yourself and become a virgin again, would you want to?"

As he looked up, I could see his tears. "Yeah, I would."

"Why, Bob?"

"Because I wish Dana could be my first."

Broken people fill my life. As a former youth pastor and now a college professor, I've heard them all—story after heartrending story. I still have not learned how to leave my work at the office.

The disturbing images that careened through my cranium that night stood in stark contrast to the two bundles of joy who eventually fell asleep on my lap. What kind of world will they face? What pressures, tensions, and temptations will lurk behind every corner, waiting to pull them in a thousand different directions? How can I possibly prepare my children to face a world in which compromise has become a way of life?

Compromise. Virtually every story related to me over the years can be inseparably linked together by one common denominator—people have subtly sold out.

The compromise of parental love and support obliterates a daughter's anticipation of her own high school graduation. Just ask Jennifer.

7

The violation of marriage vows renders the children cynical and confused as to their loyalties within the home. Just ask Mark.

The selling out of moral purity invariably spawns widespread heartache and shame. Just ask Bob.

Much of the pain people harbor today is directly traceable to compromises they have made. Many have become victimized by the compromises of those around them. From the most posh executive suite to the filthiest skid row gutter, the subtle sellout has become the order of the day.

How do we prepare our children and ourselves to live victoriously in a world characterized by such compromise? Three lines of reasoning converge to form an answer:

- We must contrast the concepts of intregrity and hypocrisy, answering the questions, "Why do people compromise?" and "What motivates others to stand firm as men and women of conviction?"

- We must clearly understand our biblical convictions, those nonnegotiable statements of truth to which we will commit our lives, regardless of the cost.

- We must practically apply these convictions to the daily situations we encounter, thus enabling us to make proper choices when the pressure to compromise becomes hot and heavy.

Written with my children in mind, motivated by the memories of countless young people with whom I have spoken, and offered for the benefit of you, my reader, *Escaping the Subtle Sellout* follows the three-point plan outlined above.

By simply reading this book, an individual will become equipped to construct his or her own set of personal convictions. A teacher will find valuable lesson material immediately transferable to the classroom. And most important, parents can use this book to build biblical convictions into the lives of their own children. All, I trust, will find *Escaping the Subtle Sellout* both stimulating and challenging.

8

Part One
Defining Our Terms

Words. They continually bombard me. At times I feel as
though I am swirling in a sea of synonyms.

Many words assault our senses every day. *Funk and
Wagnalls* notes this interesting fact: "It has been estimated
that the present English vocabulary consists of more than
one million words, including slang and dialect expressions
and scientific and technical terms, many of which only came
into use after the middle of the twentieth century. *The English vocabulary is more extensive than that of any other language in the world*" (emphasis mine).

Of course some words are far more important than
others. In fact, most people's lives have been dramatically
influenced by just a handful of words. In this section, we will
examine two potent terms: *hypocrisy* versus *integrity*.

Chapter One
THE ANATOMY OF HYPOCRISY
(Or, How to Become a Hypocrite in Three Easy Lessons)

At only two bucks a pop, the Los Angeles Zoo offers the animal lover a cornucopia of optical, auditory, and olfactory stimulations. Such a deal. Where else can you spend a memorable afternoon attending an informative lecture on the mucus membrane of the *Myrmecophaga jubata* (or Great Anteater)? And how about those ubiquitous signs?

> *Antelope,* is the common name applied to a large group of hollow-horned ruminants of the family *Bovidae,* which also includes cattle, goats, and sheep. The group comprises about 150 species, of which most are found in Africa and the remainder in Asia.

> To the uneducated, misinformed, or otherwise careless observer, the Rocky Mountain goat is often mistaken for an antelope because they share some common characteristics.

Hey, I'm sorry. I just didn't know.
     One type of sign never fails to capture my attention: the menacing skull and crossbones. It inauspiciously underscores the foreboding fact that these animals have received

11

the official designation: "Endangered species."

I checked out a comprehensive roster of all known endangered species in the world, everything from the African Wild Ass *(Equus asinus)* to the Red-cockaded Woodpecker *(Picoides borealis)*. Guess what. I discovered a glaring omission. One endangered species inexplicably did not make the list. Any ideas? I refer to a man or a woman who has no price tag attached to his or her character, individuals who refuse to sell out under any circumstances. These priceless people ought themselves to bear the mark of the skull and crossbones. These models of integrity, of whom the world is not worthy (Heb. 11:38), comprise a dwindling genus of *Homo sapiens* that has indeed become endangered.

Talk Is Cheap

A credibility crisis of massive proportions has enshrouded the church. No, I'm not beating the dead horses of the headline scandals that rocked the evangelical world in the 1980s. I am referring to the little compromises, the "subtle sellouts" which have become far too commonplace in the day-to-day interactions of God's people with their neighbors, friends, business associates, fellow students, and family members.

You know as well as I that the number one excuse people most commonly offer as a justification for rejecting Jesus Christ invariably sounds something like this: "There are just too many hypocrites in the church."

"Smoke screens," my soul-winning teacher called them. "Ignore such statements and stay on the central issue," he implored. But I have come to believe that such stinging accusations are not just "smoke screens." In fact, they are indeed the "central issues." Let's consider a few examples.

One morning the clatter of the phone shattered my concentration. On the other end of the line, my friend sounded distraught and bewildered. He obviously needed some advice.

"What's the problem, Bill?" I inquired. If only I had a dollar for every person who has told me what Bill lamented on the other end of the receiver.

"I'll never do business with a Christian again," he announced to a waiting world.

Would you like to know the gory details? Bill hired a contractor, an elder in his church no less, to build him a house. They agreed upon the price, $170,000. By the time he called me, Bill had already invested $225,000, with no end in sight. For whatever reason, a subcontractor put up the drywall before the roof was in place. "It never rains in Southern California," he explained.

Well, it did. I'm talking a torrential downpour. The deluge hit out of nowhere, decimating the interior of the house, reducing the drywall to dry rot. Bill's contractor became so exasperated, he simply walked away from the job. You talk about rubbing salt into the wounds? If you can believe it, he proceeded to slap a lien against the house for an additional $25,000. Then, he got into his car and went to his next elder's meeting.

An acquaintance of mine has worked with four realtors over the last ten years, two believers, two unbelievers. Both of the unsaved realtors conducted themselves in a thoroughly professional manner, fulfilling every promise while following through on every commitment.

How did the Christian realtors' scorecard compare? One broker told my friend to lie in order to avoid a $50 termite inspection. The other left him high-and-dry when he encountered an unexpected obstacle in his escrow, nearly costing him $11,000 in the process. What has happened to us?

Do you have any idea how many girls express to me the unconscionable fact that the unsaved guys they date often treat them with more respect than the Christian guys they have gone out with? Something has to change.

One of my colleagues recently buried his father. Reeling from the fact that his dad died an unbeliever, he turned to me for a shoulder to cry on and a listening ear.

"I witnessed to my dad on countless occasions," he confided. "He just brushed it all aside. Finally, I confronted him one day, eyeball-to-eyeball, and asked him a straightforward question—'Dad, why won't you receive Christ?'

" 'Son,' he answered, 'having been in business all these years, I've had to learn something the hard way. I have learned never to work for a Christian and never to hire one. Every time I have ever violated that principle, I ended up getting burned.' " No book on apologetics could possibly remove the mental obstacles erected by this man's experiences.

Recently, I spoke to 1,000 young people at a Christian leadership conference. These students represented the cream of the evangelical crop. I asked them this series of questions:

- How many of you personally know of a Christian marriage that ended in divorce?

- How many of you know Christians who regularly take illegal drugs?

- How many of you know Christians who rebel against their parents?

- How many of you know Christians who cheat at school?

- How many of you know Christians who are alcoholics?

- How many of you know Christians who are currently involved in an immoral sexual relationship?

- How many of you know someone who, as a Christian, got an abortion to end an unwanted pregnancy?

To every single question without exception, including the last one, the auditorium erupted into a tumultuous sea of raised hands. The youth pastors sat in stunned silence. I could have wept.

This unbelievable scene triggered within me a spontaneous and most genuine confession:

"I have been a Christian now for twenty-one years," I told them. "I know what I believe and I know why I believe it. But I must admit to you that if today I found myself sincerely searching for the truth, and in my pursuit examined all of the religions and ideologies I could find, I would reject Christianity outright as a downright fraud.

"Based upon the evidence that your raised hands have conveyed to me, I could not arrive at any other intellectually honest conclusion. As a skeptic, I would feel compelled to ask, 'What do you people have that I could possibly need or want? Your lives are no better, no different, than mine.'

"Talk is cheap, young people. If the one who claims to follow Jesus Christ does not validate his message by his lifestyle, then why should I accept his message as truth?"

Achan Stole the Bacon

The English language boasts of literally hundreds of thousands of words. A very small slice of the linguistic pie can be classified as vulgar or profane. These infamous expletives, many of which come in the four letter variety, have violated even the most pristine ears, causing them to burn with righteous indignation.

May I be so brazen as to add to the list two words of my own, just as vulgar, equally profane, as any sampling from a drunken sailor's vocabulary? *Compromise* and *hypocrisy*. Many an eternal destiny has been rocketed off course and rendered irretrievable by the tainted influences of those who have willingly succumbed to the subtle seductions represented by these words.

One man, along with his unsuspecting family, had to learn this bitter lesson the hard way. It was a lesson, by the way, that produced a ripple effect throughout an entire nation.

Do the words "under the ban" mean anything to you? They should have spoken volumes to a young soldier by the name of Achan. Have you heard of him? I wouldn't be a bit surprised if you haven't. He appears as a rather obscure bit player in the overall drama that comprises the history of Israel.

The nation had just come off a stunning victory. Inexplicably, a city's walls had come a-tumblin' down. God's army, by all indications, appeared invincible. Enemy nations cowered behind their barriers. What kind of military force could possibly have routed the mighty and fortified stronghold known as Jericho?

God's instructions regarding Jericho had been communicated only too clearly. "And the city shall be under the ban, it and all that is in it belongs to the LORD. . . . But as for you, only keep yourselves from the things *under the ban*, lest you covet them and take some of the things *under the ban*, so you would make the camp of Israel accursed and bring trouble on it" (Josh. 6:17-18, NASB, emphasis mine). You don't need a doctorate in political science to figure out what God meant.

Why did God impose this one restriction? If the soldiers ransacked the city, padding their pockets with the possessions of the people, enemy nations would conclude that the army of God was motivated by personal greed. These men were not motivated by greed. A compelling passion fueled this Middle Eastern military machine; these men jealously yearned for the manifestation of the holiness and righteousness of God in their land. At least most of them did.

As Achan entered a house in conquered Jericho, a glistening sunbeam caught his eye. Gold! One and one-quarter pounds of it, along with five pounds of silver and, for good measure, a beautiful robe. This guy must have felt as if he just won the lottery! And the fates were with him; he was all alone.

Quickly, he hid his treasures under his garment and scampered back to his tent. Finding a shovel, he dug a hole in the floor, planted the objects, and replaced the dirt. A criminologist might call this a perfect crime. No witnesses. No evidence. Nothing. His family did not even know of the sub-terranean cache concealed beneath their feet.

After conquering Jericho, Commander-in-chief Joshua consulted his military advisers and determined that 3,000 men could easily take the city of Ai. Most maps represent Ai with a pinpoint. If you were looking for a thriving metropolis, Ai was just not the place.

When the citizens of Ai unexpectedly rose up against the best of Israel's army, 36 Israelite soldiers died. The remaining 2,900+ panicked and ran for their lives. God's reputation disintegrated overnight. The work of God hit a wall.

"Israel has sinned" (Josh. 7:11) became the banner cry throughout the camp. Indeed, the compromise of one always destroys the corporate credibility of the many.

Joshua received some very intriguing instructions. God could have simply pointed out the guilty party. But He didn't. God chose to use this "teachable moment" to imprint upon the minds of His people the dire consequences of the subtle sellout.

God instructed Joshua to select a member from each of the twelve tribes of Israel, twelve men who would subsequently march in front of their leader. In full view of the entire nation, guess whose tribe was recognized as guilty?

This major media event continued as one member from each of the clans from within Achan's tribe appeared before Joshua. Achan's clan received the nod.

Now a representative from each of the families from within the clan mounted the steps of the platform. The gaze of the entire nation fell upon Achan, his wife, and his children.

God began with a searchlight, then gradually and methodically compressed it into a laser beam and aimed it directly at the guilty party. Just from a logistical standpoint, this must have taken hours. What nightmarish thoughts must have undulated through Achan's grey matter all this time? Surely he must have known that he would soon be unmasked. Yet, and here's the point—throughout this entire process, Achan kept his big mouth shut. He purposely presented himself to his family and to his nation as *something different* than what he knew he was. We have on our hands a world-class hypocrite.

Each member of Achan's family marched across the platform. Slowly and deliberately, Achan made his way up the stairs. Wouldn't you just love to read his mind at this point? He must have felt like a terrorist approaching a metal detector at LAX or JFK, praying all the while that the alarm would not sound. But sound it did.

The Bible records the most profound events in such concise terminology. "Joshua had [Achan's] family come forward man by man, and Achan . . . was taken" (Josh. 7:18). Unmasked, naked unto the world, guilty as charged.

The Anatomy of Hypocrisy

Would you like to learn how to become a hypocrite in three easy lessons? Listen to Achan as he "repents." "It is true! I have sinned against the LORD, the God of Israel" (Josh. 1:20). That was a news bulletin! "This is what I have done: (1) I saw the robe, the silver, and the gold. (2) I coveted them. (3) I took them" (Josh. 7:20-21).

I honestly believe that had the story ended here, Achan could have confessed his crime, produced the bootlegged bathrobe, et al., and the incident would have been forgiven and forgotten. But Achan did something more. And when he did it, he crossed the demilitarized zone into the booby-trapped minefield of hypocrisy. He *buried* the spoils.

The questions before the house are these: "Is anything buried in our lives? Anything hidden? Anything covered? Are we consciously presenting ourselves to our families and friends as one kind of person, knowing all the while that we are totally different than the perceptions we try so hard to create?" If so, Numbers 32:23 ought to keep us awake at night—"You may be sure that your sin will find you out."

So what happened to Achan? "Joshua said, 'Why have you brought this disaster on us? The LORD will bring disaster on you today.' Then all Israel stoned [Achan], and after they had stoned the rest [of his family], they burned them. Over Achan they heaped up a large pile of rocks, which remains to this day" (Josh. 7:26). That stone monument stood as a persuasive reminder of God's absolute hatred of the subtle sellout.

Taking Inventory

Are You for Sale?

1. Write down your immediate reactions and responses to this chapter. What were your first impressions? What went through your mind as you read?

2. In a concordance, look up the word *hypocrite* and its derivatives. Read each verse or passage in your Bible. Record your findings on a chart. Your chart might look like this:

Passage	Description of Hypocrisy	Consequences of Hypocrisy
Matt. 23:23	Focus on externals; neglect the internal attitudes of the heart	Condemned by God "Woe to you"
Matt. 23:24	Blind to real issues	Lead many people astray
Matt. 23:25	Unaware of the condition of their own hearts	Corruption from the inside out
Etc.		

3. Based on your research, formulate your own definition of hypocrisy.

4. Apply your definition to your own life. Honestly answer

the question, "Have I compromised what I know to be right?"

5. Read Matthew 5:23-24. Whom have you violated in the process of your compromise? What steps must you take in order to clear the slate? Must any restitution be made? How about another chart?

Person violated	Nature of Offense	Steps I Must Take	Date Completed
1.			
2.			
3.			
Etc.			

If you sincerely cannot think of anyone you have violated, try to remember some people from the past and the steps you took to right the situation. Then move to number 7.

6. Set some time goals for approaching those whom you have offended. Humbly identify what you did, along with the wrong attitude you may have communicated. Then ask the all-important question, "Will you forgive me?" while making any necessary restitution.

7. After completing the chart in number 5, share with your family members the lessons you have learned through this process of correcting your compromises. Allow yourself to become vulnerable as you express to them the pain you experienced when the truth of your hypocrisy hit you for the first time. Contrast your hurt with the joy that resulted from doing the right thing.

Relate to them the responses of the people as you asked for forgiveness, even if an individual responded wrongly. There are no guarantees that all stories will have a happy ending. Stress the fact that we are all people in process. It may take time for certain individuals to accept an apology. This will prepare the members of your family for any wrong responses they might encounter.

Chapter Two:
THE ENVY OF THE WICKED
(Or, How to Become a Man or Woman of INTEGRITY in Three Easy Lessons)

Have you ever pondered the possibility of someone discovering the actual, physical body of Jesus, thereby disproving the Resurrection? Oh, it'll never happen. But if it did, Christianity would crumble like a house of cards.

Think of the pressures such a disclosure would relieve. Please don't misunderstand me. I would not trade one second of my life now for all of the first seventeen years of my life that I lived without Christ. But let's face the facts. The Christian life does carry some enormous pressures. Why else would Paul write, "If only for this life we have hope in Christ, we are to be pitied more than all men"? (1 Cor. 15:19)

You want to talk pressure? Boy, have we got some pressure. Just try these on for size.

- Christians have been called by God to an unfailing commitment to an ethical standard that requires superhuman strength to maintain (1 Peter 1:15-16).

- Our words, actions, attitudes, and motives must be held continually in check (Rom. 14:10-12).

- We live in a toxic cultural environment which arouses our bombarded senses to the point where they scream for fulfillment (1 John 2:15-16).

- Yet, we must daily deny ourselves even the slightest opportunity for sensual gratification (1 Cor. 15:31).

- We fight an unseen enemy, a myriad of fallen angels dedicated to our total destruction (1 Peter 5:8).

- A watching world waits in eager expectation, ready to spring to a standing ovation every time one of our ranks struggles, stumbles, and falls (John 17:14).

Here's the kicker. As if these pressures were not enough, every one of us finds ourselves surrounded by people completely unfettered as far as their lifestyle is concerned. They can go wherever their little heart desires, and do whatever they want, whenever they want, with whomever they want. And, contrary to much of the preaching I have received over the years, they are having a blast.

A Fleeting Fantasy

May I be embarrassingly transparent with you for a moment? At times I find myself getting a little jealous of some of my unsaved friends. What would it be like to live my life with absolutely no restraints? No wonder Solomon warned us in unmistakable terms, "Do not let your heart envy sinners, but always be zealous for the fear of the LORD" (Prov. 23:17).

My depraved desire to chuck the "Christian scene" rears its ugly head on the rarest of occasions. I can probably count on one hand the number of times I have faced the seduction of such fleeting fantasies in the two decades that I have been a believer. Yet, my "envy of the wicked" can feel overwhelming at times.

One notable example took place in one of my favorite establishments of gourmet delights—McDonald's. Anything beats camp food, right? My son and I had existed on fruit loops and macaroni and cheese until our bellies bellowed for a reprieve. We both found ourselves suffering from a common form of malnutrition, popularly designated "The Big Mac Attack." Please don't tell anyone, but under the cloak of darkness, while braving subfreezing temperatures, David and I sneaked out of camp to the nearby golden arches beckoning for our patronage.

While settling into our booth, we fingered the sesame seed buns, anxiously anticipating the delectable delicacy our palates were about to embrace. Suddenly, the side door opened and eight skiers romped in. The four guys and four girls sat in the booth adjacent to ours. Never one to pass up the opportunity to find a good illustration, I tuned my antenna in their direction.

"What a great day!" one of them blurted.

"Conditions couldn't have been better," another agreed.

After a few minutes of this, the girls excused themselves and went to wherever girls go when they leave the table in pairs. In their absence, the men did a most curious thing. They went through a little ritual to determine which guy would pair up with which girl in the cabin that night.

Suddenly life seemed quite unfair to me. Momentarily, I would flush down my cholesterol cuisine with a large diet coke, return to the camp, and speak to 350 junior highers, half of whom couldn't care less about anything I had to say.

All the while, four guys would grab their six-packs, head up a snow-covered hill on this moonlit night of enchantment, snuggle up next to a crackling fire with the girl of their choice, and enjoy a night of unbridled ecstasy and fantasy.

Something whispered into my ear, "Dewey, old boy, you're a fool. You are being royally ripped off."

Confessions of a Choir Director

Don't let my confession shock you too much. Asaph expressed the identical sentiment in the seventy-third Psalm.

While his picture never appeared on the cover of *Christianity Today,* make no mistake about it; Asaph was no spiritual slouch. He led one of the temple choirs. King David handpicked Asaph's sons for the ministry of prophesying.

Asaph himself "prophesied under the king's supervision" (1 Chron. 25:2). And for good measure, Asaph authored a grand total of twelve psalms.

As you listen to these "confessions of a choir director" ask yourself if you can relate to his lament:

> Surely God is good to Israel, to those who are pure in heart. But as for me, my feet had almost slipped; I had nearly lost my foothold. For I envied the arrogant when I saw the prosperity of the wicked. They have no struggles; their bodies are healthy and strong" (Ps. 73:1-4).

Listen to the mockery of the wicked as they challenge God to pay the slightest attention to their rebellious lifestyles:

> They say, "How can God know? Does the Most High have knowledge?" This is what the wicked are like— always carefree, they increase in wealth" (vv. 11-12).

Asaph's conclusion sounds most pathetic:

> Surely in vain have I kept my heart pure; in vain have I washed my hands in innocence. All day long I have been plagued; I have been punished every morning" (vv. 13-14).

In other words, given my situation, I might declare: "For twenty-one years I have lived an absolutely pure life. For what? What have I received in return? Nothing. Nothing but the agonizing pressure of trying to maintain a commitment to a God I cannot see, in the midst of a world that hates me and everything I stand for. Have I been ripped off?"

But It's Not Supposed to Work This Way

A student recently asked me a provocative question. "What has kept you going through all these years of ministry?"

My answer? "I've had enough successes in the ministry to keep me motivated, but enough failures to keep me humble." Let me share with you three of my most painful failures.

I led "Brian" to Christ when he was a junior in high school. You talk about a transformed life—Brian redefined the term. After graduation he attended a very fine Christian college, preparing himself to become a missionary. While in school he met a peach of a girl who shared his vision. They married shortly after his college graduation.

Brian loved sports. He knew the statistics of every team. He discovered that he could predict the outcomes of major sporting events with an uncanny accuracy. He started placing little wagers on certain games and won. He then decided to place bets for his friends as long as he could have "a piece of the action." Before long, Brian built up a rather lucrative business. He eventually became a full-time bookie.

I called him one day and asked about his plans to go to the mission field. "On hold," he replied curtly. I asked him to reconcile for me his newly chosen "career" with his commitment to Christ. He exploded. "Back off," he demanded. "What's wrong with a guy making a little money?"

I hung up the receiver and slumped into my chair, burying my head in my hands. *Have I been wrong all these years?* I asked myself. *Maybe Brian's right. What is wrong with a guy making a little money from something he so obviously enjoys?*

At twenty-one years of age "Steve" demonstrated the potential to become one of the best communicators I knew. I hired him as an intern so that I could personally pour my life into his.

Everything went along swimmingly until the "Beach, Barbecue, Burnout." A new girl came along, met Steve, and things began to sizzle with excitement. Cupid's arrow hit the bull's-eye. They walked along the beach together. Innocent enough, right? They held hands on the long walk back. OK, so it's a free country. When I yelled over to Steve to start packing up, he gave her a little kiss on the cheek. Hmmm. I made a mental note for future reference.

A couple of weeks later, I asked him about "Sue." When he immediately broke eye contact with me, I knew I had hit a dangling nerve ending. He became evasive, irritated, exasperated, and then infuriated.

"Why are you getting so upset, Steve? You are not sleeping with her are you?"

"And what if I am?" he fired back. "What are you going to do about it? Listen, you are looking at a happy man."

Those words sliced into me like a meat cleaver. *Have I been wrong all these years?* I wondered slightly. *It's not supposed to work that way. For years I've preached, "You'll reap what you sow. Sexual immorality will come back to bite you big time. Keep yourselves pure." How can Steve refer to himself as a "happy man"?*

Jackie married her high school sweetheart. "Cheerleader Marries Football Star," the headlines might read. "John" came to Christ in my backyard Bible study. Jackie and John both went away to college, returned after four years, and rekindled the relationship. It didn't take long for John to pop the question. They asked me to officiate at what promised to be the social event of the year. (Oh, yes, we're talking "The Mother of All Weddings" here!)

Her mother called me just about a year later. "My daughter wants to leave him," she shared through her tears. "She has friends making $50,000 a year while she's stuck at home being a housewife. She's scared to death that she'll get pregnant and spend the rest of her life changing Pampers. Besides, she's bored with her marriage." I opened my mouth, but no words came out. What could I possibly say?

Jackie and John exemplified the kind of teaching I gave my youth group week after week, year after year. They did everything right. And Jackie got bored.

My soul-searching began again. Did I deceive them? Have I led them astray? Maybe she's just not cut out to be a mother and a housewife. Maybe making fifty grand a year isn't so bad. Maybe, if I was completely honest with myself, I would have to admit that at times I feel bored. Perhaps I've ripped them off. Perhaps, in the process, I have been ripped off myself.

The Anatomy of Integrity

Please don't put this book down yet. I have some very good news for you. Remember McDonald's? I did not go to the skiers' cabin that night. (They might have thought it pretty strange if I did!) My son and I finished our Big Macs, chug-a-lugged our diet Cokes, and returned to the camp. Aren't you glad? In fact, looking back over my life as a Christian, I have never once given in to my envy of the wicked.

Neither did Asaph. He stands today in marked contrast to the likes of an Achan. Oh, yes, he felt the pressure. The disillusionments brought on by the seemingly incontrovertible evidence swirled through his mind. "These fat cats have everything their hearts could ever wish for!" he bemoaned. "And so God's people are dismayed and confused" (Ps. 73:7, 10, TLB), he bewailed. Wasn't he talking here about himself? Yet, Asaph's convictions won the day!

Asaph maintained his integrity, his personal commitment to excellence of character. He did not compromise. He may have teetered on the precipice, but he did not sell out. I will let Asaph himself explain why.

"I would have betrayed Your [God's] children" (Ps. 73:15).

If we give in to our envy of the wicked, how many people will we betray? If we fall into compromise, how many others will fall with us? How many people are directly or indirectly affected by our lifestyles? How many individuals look to us as examples?

Recently, I made my daily trek to my mailbox at the college and discovered within the small steel cocoon a copy of this poem, placed there by one of my students:

The lecture you deliver may be very wise and true,
but I'd rather get my lesson by observing what you do.
For I might misunderstand you, and the high advice you give.
But there's no misunderstanding how you act and how you live.

At the bottom of the page Kimberley wrote: "Thank you, Dewey, for not just telling me how to live, but for showing me how to live. I will never forget it." If I went down, how many of my students would I take down with me? I'd take Kimberley down, for sure.

A camper wrote me a letter in which she told me about her youth pastor who resigned after a several month affair with a girl in his youth group. In her last paragraph, Angie wrote in big, bold, capital letters, "Dewey, please don't let me down. You are the only hope I've got that Christianity is real." I don't know about you, but I don't need that kind of pressure.

A middle-aged man walked up to me in a grocery store and gave me a bear hug, right in front of the kumquats! Rich introduced himself and explained that he had brought his twenty-five-year-old son and seventy-year-old father to a Father-Son camp at which I recently spoke. Both had prayed with me to receive Christ. His eyes welled up with tears as he added, "Just last week, my dad went to be with Jesus. If it weren't for you . . . " his voice trailed off as he squeezed me even tighter. How could I ever let Rich down?

If you asked my son, "David, what do you want to be when you grow up?" he would square his shoulders and proudly declare, "I want to be just like my dad." How could I ever let him down?

How about my little Ashley, who has made me her

hero? Or Becky, the dear woman who took a big risk when she committed the rest of her life to me as my wife? How could I ever betray their trust?

"Then I understood their final destiny. . . . How suddenly are they destroyed!" (Ps. 73:17-19).

For all of their "fun in the sun," have "the wicked" considered the price tag? "Do not be deceived: God cannot be mocked. A man reaps what he sows. The one who sows to please his sinful nature, from that nature will reap destruction" (Gal. 6:7-8).

A lot of people might feel differently about demanding their rights to live any way they please if they had to spend their time like I do—picking up the pieces. In my counseling ministry I have had to learn a very painful lesson. You might want to call this "Humpty Dumpty Theology:"

Humpty Dumpty sat on a wall;
Humpty Dumpty had a great fall;
And all the king's horses and all the king's men
Couldn't put Humpty Dumpty back together again.

Sometimes the scars of our rebellion last a lifetime. Sometimes the consequences of our disobedience may be eternal. The words, "And they lived happily ever after," do not always apply.

Consider for a moment the "benefits" experienced by those eight skiers spending a moonlight night in a cozy cabin on a snow covered hillside. For a one-time sexual encounter, these young people may have effectively:

- sowed the seeds of distrust which may ultimately undermine a future marriage;
- forfeited any semblance of a genuine and lasting intimacy of heart and soul;
- scarred their own souls by searing their consciences;

- contributed dramatically to the moral breakdown of our nation;

- conceived an innocent, unwanted child;

- become some of the 35,000 Americans per day who receive any one of 52 sexually transmitted diseases, many of which produce cancer, several of which remain incurable, and one which inevitably kills its victims;

- further enslaved themselves to the sinful passions of their flesh;

- and been given over to depraved minds with which they can no longer distinguish between right and wrong.

For what? A fading memory of a few-seconds-long tingle?

I know of one girl who, at the age of nineteen, had sex for the first time in her life. During that "one night stand" she contracted genital herpes, a disease for which there is no cure. Several years later, she met a man whom she genuinely loved and eventually married. After passing genital herpes on to her husband, she discovered to her own horror that her three week old baby girl had become infected with herpes as well. A pretty hefty price to pay for a goosebump, wouldn't you say? You tell me who's been ripped off.

"I was senseless and ignorant" (Ps. 73:22).

Why? Because in the final analysis, the wicked do not have anything we need nor could truly want. Invariably they end up with a handful of bubbles.

I'll never forget buying my son his first bottle of bubbles. He blew those babies and oohed and aahed as he watched them dangle in space. As their slimy surfaces refracted the sunlight into a rainbow of colors, he wanted to reach out and play with them.

David became the picture of frustration every time he grasped one of those slithery spheroids, only to open his hand and find out that he held firmly on to nothing. Grabbing the little wand, he blew a hundred more and lashed at the air, desperately trying to take his first bubble captive. But alas, just when he thought he had enclosed his fingers around another floating ball, pop. As Vin Scully, the Hall of Fame announcer for the Los Angeles Dodgers, once said, in describing a shortstop who let a routine ground ball roll under his glove, "He just came up with a handful of empty."

I cannot think of a better description of the wicked. Just when they think they have found something that will ultimately satisfy their fleshly cravings, pop. What did eight skiers get in a cabin that night? Bubbles. Handfuls of empty.

"Being with you, I desire nothing on earth" (Ps. 73:25).

Only a relationship with God can ultimately satisfy.

- Enoch walked with God. That was enough (Gen. 5:24).

- Moses sang, "The LORD is my strength and my song" (Ex. 15:2).

- David prayed, "You have made known to me the path of life [Not just an empty existence, but life!]; You will fill me with joy in Your presence, with eternal pleasures at Your right hand" (Ps. 16:11).

- Solomon instructed, "Fear God and keep His commandments, for this is the whole duty of man" (Ecc. 12:13).

- Mary sang, "My soul glorifies the Lord and my spirit rejoices in God my Savior" (Luke 1:46-47).

- Paul admitted, "I consider everything a loss compared to the surpassing greatness of knowing Christ Jesus my Lord" (Phil. 3:8).

- Peter reminded his readers that God's "divine power has given us everything we need for life . . . through our knowledge of Him" (2 Peter 1:3).

- John boasted, "The world and its desires pass away, but the man who does the will of God lives forever" (1 John 2:17).

- Asaph concluded our discussion so beautifully:

Whom have I in heaven but You? And being with You, I desire nothing on earth. My flesh and my heart may fail, but God is the strength of my heart and my portion forever. . . . it is good to be near God" (Ps. 73:25-28).

Remember "Brian," the would-be missionary turned bookie? I lost touch with him until a few years ago.

"Brian! How are you doing?"

"Oh, I guess you haven't heard. My wife left me about a year ago. She got tired of living with a hypocrite. I'm all alone."

I said something really profound like, "Well, at least you're making a lot of money, right?"

"Yeah, right," he sneered. "You want to know something? Everything I ever bought broke."

Who got ripped off?

My former intern "Steve" walked out of my life after his beach romance. When I finally saw him again years later, I did a double take. He had lost all of his hair. "Hey Steve, boy it's good to see you. How's Sue?" I inquired.

"Oh, I guess you haven't heard? She left me not too long ago. She met another guy on the beach."

"Well, umm, how are you doing otherwise?" I stumbled.

"Haven't you heard? I was recently diagnosed as having terminal cancer. I've only got six months to live."

Who got ripped off?

Married to her high school sweetheart, Jackie wanted her own "piece of the action." She filed for a divorce, leaving John to refer to her as "my very own Judas." When I looked into his eyes recently, I saw a man who had become utterly defeated, disillusioned, cynical, and bitter. Understandably so.

I ran into Jackie's mom just the other day. "How's Jackie doing?" I asked.

Through her tears she said, "Dewey, it is so hard. She went back East to start her career, but things just didn't work out. She had an affair with her boss and ended up on the street. Now she's living in some sleazy apartment with a couple of other girls while working as a cocktail waitress at a truck stop."

Who got ripped off?

Do not let your heart envy sinners, but always be zealous for the fear of the LORD. There is surely a future hope for you, and your hope will not be cut off" (Prov. 23:17-18).

Taking Inventory

Are You for Sale?

1. As you look back over your life, can you recall instances in which you envied the wicked? If so, list the times, the reasons for your envy, your responses, and the outcome.

2. In this chapter I mentioned several people in my life who chose a path of rebellion, and then I recalled the devastating consequences that resulted. Can you do the same? Such examples can serve as compelling object lessons to motivate you and your children to maintain biblical convictions regardless of the cost.

3. As an interesting study, take your children through the Book of Proverbs, one chapter per day. Mark each reference that contains the words *wicked, sinners,* or any related term.

Record the consequences that befall such people.

4. Now trace the concept of *righteousness* or *obedience* through the Book of Proverbs. How does God bless the lives of those who follow Him? What are their reasons for living in obedience?

5. Do you read a daily newspaper? The overwhelming majority of articles vividly illustrate the consequences that result when people choose a path of rebellion rather than obedience to God. Begin to relate biblical truth to the headlines of the day. This exercise will cause the Word to come alive and explode with relevance.

6. Young people need heroes. Unfortunately, they typically turn to the wrong people—rock stars, prominent athletes, etc. How about introducing your children to a whole new group of potential heroes? Begin to read them the lively biographies of some of God's choice servants. As you do, underscore the right choices each one made in fleshing out his or her commitment to Jesus Christ. Emphasize the lasting benefit that has come to our lives, the world as a whole, and the kingdom of God because of their righteous dedication.

7. Become a hero to your children. Each time you are tempted with an opportunity to envy the wicked, relate the circumstances to your children along with your reasons for standing firm. Whenever you choose a righteous path, let them know why. Remember, effective parenting is in reality effective modeling.

Part Two
Establishing Our Convictions

The Scriptures are filled with glowing examples of men and women of integrity. Joseph "refused" the sensuous seductions of another man's wife by asking, "How then could I do such a wicked thing and sin against God?" (Gen. 39:9) "Esther sent this reply to Mordecai: 'If I perish, I perish' " (Es. 4:16). "Daniel resolved not to defile himself" (Dan. 1:8). "Shadrach, Meschach and Abednego replied to the king . . . 'We will not serve your gods' " (Dan. 3:16-18).

We want desperately to join their ranks, do we not? Such a quest begins when we develop our own set of convictions and then teach them diligently to our children. In order to illustrate this concept most clearly, I shall now make reference to my own list of biblical nonnegotiables. You may choose to adopt them for your family, or to use them to spur your thinking as you develop your own.

Chapter Three:
UNDER NEW MANAGEMENT

Conviction #1—Jesus Christ alone rules the universe;
therefore, Jesus Christ alone rules my life
(Philippians 2:10-11).

"Hey, get this straight. I may have accepted Christ at that camp last month, but there's no way He's going to control my life." High-school-aged middle linebackers can often provide rich examples of gross theological aberrations, I'll admit, but this guy missed it by a mile. As I fill you in on the details, place this one under the category, "Could this be my kid someday?"

The story begins at a high school summer camp, two weeks before Hoover High's infamous "Hell Week," a torturous five days of relentless practice. In response to the speaker's inspirational anecdote about Jesus "turning losers into winners," several players from the varsity football team made "decisions" to receive Christ. Lucky me, the next Sunday morning they all showed up at my Sunday School class.

"Great to see you here," I greeted them. "Why did you guys decide to come?"

They awkwardly looked back and forth at each other while shuffling their feet and clearing their throats. Finally, one of the players squared his shoulders, mustered up all of the courage in the world, and announced, "We all just became Christians!" to which the others nodded and said, "Yeah, that's it, we just became Christians."

"Oh," I said. "And just why did you do that?"

Without a moment's hesitation, one player blurted out, "Because with God on our team we can't lose."

"Ah huh," I said, trying my best to conceal my cynicism. "I guess we'll just see, won't we?"

That dialogue took place on a Sunday morning. A couple of weeks later, one of the girls in my youth group, a Hoover High cheerleader no less, stopped dead in her tracks when she saw our middle linebacker friend standing in front of a neighbor's house. A party was in full swing, and this guy was stone drunk. At least I guess he was. How else can we explain his unorthodox behavior? Melinda saw him urinating on his friend's parked car.

"What are you doing here?" she questioned. "I thought you became a Christian." He promptly responded with the terse doctrinal distortion with which I began this chapter.

Well, guess what happened? Hoover lost seven of their first eight games. Apparently Jesus forgot to suit up. In retrospect, it seems that the faithfulness of each team member's Sunday School attendance became inversely proportional to their number of losses. By the end of the season, I would defy you to find one football player within ten miles of my church on a Sunday morning.

While the details of this scenario may seem a bit unusual, I can assure you that our football player/party goer's theological orientation is far from the exception. His doctrinal data base allowed him to completely compartmentalize his Christianity. He successfully divorced his commitment to Christ from every other aspect of his life. He thereby displayed an "anything goes" morality devoid of any twinge of conscience. What will prevent my children, or yours for that matter, from someday doing the same?

Our churches are frighteningly full of "middle linebacker theologians." I recently saw an interesting reminder of this syndrome. On the left bumper of a car a sticker read, "Give Jesus a chance." On the right bumper another sticker contained a four letter synonym for the words *human excrement* followed by the verb *happens.* Consistency, thou art a rare jewel!

How does this happen? Tragically, too many people "receive" Jesus Christ for the *wrong* reasons. Let's get even more basic. Many people, even many professing Christians, do not understand who Jesus is, why Jesus came, or what Jesus demands. As parents, we must insure that our own children never fall into this category!

A Glimmer of Hope

Hope indeed burns eternal! One summer I had the distinct privilege of helping to lead a study tour in Israel. I witnessed something on that trip which would warm the cockles of any parent's heart. On a sunny summer's afternoon our tour group gathered on the bank of the Jordan River for a baptismal service. The pastor doing the actual baptizing allowed each person to give a personal testimony of his relationship with Christ.

Then came the climax. The pastor's ten-year-old son waded into the water and stood to face the crowd. His testimony was short, sweet, and most sincere. "I don't know what I'm going to be when I grow up," he admitted. "But one thing's for sure. I am going to be whatever Jesus wants me to be." I know one middle linebacker I wish could have heard those words. And with that, his father proudly lowered his son into the water.

Needless to say, that sight brought tears to my eyes. Hope does indeed burn eternal. Even within our secularized society, we as parents *can* effectively pass on to our children the proper conviction regarding Jesus Christ:

Jesus Christ alone rules the universe; therefore Jesus Christ alone rules my life (Phil. 2:10-11).

How can we as parents build this nonnegotiable into

the lives and hearts of our own children? The answer hinges upon the single most important question ever uttered on this planet.

Jesus phrased this question Himself. The eternal destinies of multiplied billions of people hang upon their response to His words: "What do you think about the Christ? Whose son is He?" (Matt. 22:42) How would our children answer this question?

Misguided Motivations

A high-school-aged middle linebacker certainly wasn't the first to give a bogus answer to Jesus' inquiry. Check out the sobering scene that unfolds on the blustery shores of the Sea of Galilee as recorded in John 6.

Crowds were nothing new to Jesus. News of Him ricocheted throughout the neighborhoods at lightning speed. In John's account we read that "a great crowd of people followed Him" (John 6:2). When He sat down with His disciples, "Jesus looked up and saw a great crowd coming toward Him" (v. 5). The next day, the crowd got into the boats and went to Capernaum in search of Jesus" (v. 24).

How puzzling, then, to read: "Many of His disciples turned back and no longer followed Him. 'You do not want to leave too, do you?' Jesus asked the Twelve" (vv. 66-67).

What a difference a day makes. Jesus went from throngs of people, numbering close to 20,000, to a mere handful of 12 individuals — and all this in just under sixty-six verses! Today, if a pastor started with 12 and ended up with 20,000, we'd give him an honorary doctorate and make him the keynote speaker at every pastor's conference in the country. Yet, if anyone started with 20,000 and, after preaching one sermon, ended up with only 12, he'd be fired overnight! Have we gotten our priorities twisted somewhere along the way?

What went wrong? In this case, as happens all too frequently to churchgoers today, thousands of people followed Jesus, spurred on by their own misguided motivations. They "received" Jesus, all right, but they received Him for the wrong reasons.

Some people followed Him because of His miracles. "A great crowd of people followed Him because they saw the miraculous signs He had performed on the sick" (v. 2). They reduced Jesus to a genie in bottle—ready, willing, and able to grant them any three wishes their selfish hearts desired. They viewed Jesus merely as a magic man and nothing more.

Some people followed Him because of His political potential. "Jesus, knowing that they intended to come and make Him king by force, withdrew again to a mountain by Himself" (v. 15). "Down with Caesar!" became the battle cry of the people. "Overthrow Rome!" became the one plank in their party's political platform. They sought a benevolent dictator who could smash the ironfisted rule of Rome and usher in a utopian existence. Jesus became their ticket to "the good life" of ease and comfort. Unfortunately for them, Jesus refused to declare His candidacy.

Some people simply wanted another free lunch. "Jesus answered, 'You are looking for Me . . . because you ate the loaves and had your fill' " (v. 26). The masses perceived Jesus to be a walking welfare system, and that was good enough for them.

Put it all together and what do you get? A first century sampling of a modern day doctrinal deviation. Prosperity theology abounds today, in both fundamental and charismatic circles, just as it did in Jesus' day. "Come to Jesus," the preacher beckons. "He'll make you healthy (the people saw the miraculous signs He had performed on the sick), wealthy (they ate the loaves and had their fill), and happy (they intended to make him king by force)." Sound familiar? I hear a resounding echo bouncing off the walls of my Sunday School classroom saying something like this: "Because with God on our team, we can't lose." Déjà vu, my friend.

Please don't make the mistake of writing off my football example as an extreme case of adolescent naïveté. I've heard too many adults express the exact same sentiments, filtered through their own grid of grown-up concerns. When a friend of mine, a teacher at a fine Christian school, recounted for me the disappointment she faced because something didn't quite go her way, she said to me in a defiant tone of voice, "Yeah, God and I are going at it right now. The Christian life just isn't supposed to be this way." And wouldn't you know that I was the first person she called when her son walked away from Jesus Christ. She blamed the church's youth group. "Not enough activities," she told me. "No wonder he lost interest." I've got a sneaking suspicion that perhaps he lost interest for a totally different reason.

Mortal Miscalculations

One element in the biblical accounts we just looked at is most unnerving. On the surface the people sounded so sincere, even to the point of asking the right questions. However, they made one fatal mistake: They miscalculated who Jesus really is.

"What must we do to do the works God requires?" they asked (v. 28). Not a bad start, right?

"What miraculous sign then will You give that we may see it and believe You?" they continued (v. 30). They did not want to commit their lives to just any guru who came down the pike. You can't fault them for that.

"Sir . . . from now on give us this bread" (v. 34). They displayed an intense hunger in their hearts. This gang seemed ripe for the picking. But outward appearances can be most deceiving, can't they? I wonder if any high-school-aged middle linebackers were lurking in their midst?

How did Jesus respond to His "read" of the crowd? How should anyone respond to those who have become hardened by their misguided motivations and mortal miscalculations? Jesus preached one scorcher of a sermon. He pulled no punches. With surgical precision, He drove His "sword of the Spirit" (Eph. 6:17) deep into the heretical hearts of His followers, exposing their miscalculations for what they really were.

They miscalculated who Jesus is.

Then Jesus declared, "I am the bread of life. My Father's will is that everyone who looks to the Son and believes in Him shall have eternal life, and I will raise him up at the last day" (vv. 35, 40).

Far more than being a magical man who went about the countryside merrily distributing free food, Jesus is God.

The moment Jesus opened His mouth, He had a captive audience. "At this the Jews began to grumble about Him because He said, 'I am the bread that came down from heaven' " (v. 41).

Why the reaction? Emphasis should *not* be placed on the *bread.* He merely used that metaphor to describe Himself as the true provider and sustainer of life. So far so good. He did not rattle their cages by using a homespun comparison, I can assure you.

Do you see the two little words *I am?* Twenty-three times in the Gospel of John, Jesus refers to Himself thus. Every Jew in town knew exactly what He meant. Those words, taken from Exodus 3:14, constitute God's unique name, reserved exclusively for Himself. No mere mortal would dare utter that name in reference to himself. Such presumption would constitute sheer blasphemy. Make no mistake about it, Jesus claimed to be Almighty God.

Note the reaction of the crowd. "Is this not Jesus, the son of *Joseph,* whose father and mother we know? How can He now say, '*I came down from heaven'?*" (v. 42, emphasis mine)

My wife and I will never forget the first memory verse our daughter ever quoted. If you can tolerate a smidgeon of fatherly bragging, my little Ashley said it word perfect! "Thou God seest me." She even knew the reference —

Jennifer 16:13! That's exactly who Jesus is—the God of the universe, who sees our every move and sovereignly orchestrates the events in our lives in accordance with His perfect plan (Rom. 12:2). For whatever reason, those in the crowd that day seemed to miss the obvious.

They miscalculated why Jesus came.

I am the living bread that came down from heaven. If anyone eats of this bread, he will live forever. This bread is My flesh, which I will give for the life of the world (v. 51).

"Then the Jews began to argue sharply among themselves, 'How can this man give us his flesh to eat?' (v. 52). They didn't get it, did they? They were still thinking about their stomachs, when all the while they should have been thinking about their souls. Much to their disappointment, Jesus did not come to satisfy their earthly appetites, their hunger for comfort, their desire for a life of ease. And He also did not come to satisfy a linebacker's passion for winning football games. He came for an infinitely more profound and important reason, which He makes clear a little later in His message.

They miscalculated what Jesus demands.

Whoever eats My flesh and drinks My blood has eternal life, and I will raise him up at the last day. . . . The one who feeds on Me will live because of Me (vv. 54, 57).

Do Jesus' words sound a bit like an endorsement for wholesale cannibalism? What kind of statement is this, "Whoever eats My flesh and drinks My blood?"

Remember, He is weaving the metaphor throughout the entire fabric of His sermon. Understanding this, the illustration becomes crystal clear. "Anyone who follows Me must be as committed to Me and as dependent upon Me, in a spiritual sense, as he is to food in a physical sense" (my paraphrase). Just as food nourishes, sustains, and energizes our physical bodies, so our lives must be nourished, sustained, and energized by Jesus Christ Himself.

Jesus' statement constituted nothing less than a call to total commitment. No wonder some gagged on His words. "On hearing it, many of His disciples said, 'This is a hard teaching. Who can accept it?' " (v. 60).

The result? After reading the fine print in the contract, the vast majority of Jesus' followers concluded that a commitment to Christ simply cost too much. "From this time many of His disciples turned back and no longer followed Him" (v. 66).

The same thing happens today with an alarming frequency. Recently, a former student confessed to me that she had grown tired of the constraints placed on her by her Baptist upbringing. "I wanted to see more, do more, and get more out of life. So what's wrong with that?"

She began innocently enough—just an occasional beer with her friends. That led to wine coolers and parties. She met a guy who swept her off her feet, a new and exhilarating experience for her. *We'll just be friends,* she told herself. Famous last words. She and I are meeting again. She desperately needs my counsel. It seems that her "friend" date-raped her on New Year's Eve.

Peter's Proclamation

In response to one of the most poignant questions of Jesus' earthly ministry, "You do not want to leave too, do you?" (v. 67), Peter rushed to the rescue, setting the record straight:

Lord, to whom shall we go? You have the words of eternal life. We believe and know that You are the Holy One of God (vv. 68-69).

What a profound statement. In a mere twenty-five words Peter confronted and corrected each of the three miscalculations of the crowd. His statement needs to be reiterated today. These words should be etched in wood, framed, and hung in every home for parents and children to consider every day. We shall consider the elements of his statement in reverse order.

Peter understood exactly who Jesus is— "The Holy One of God."

Those words—*The Holy One*—zero in on the crowning attribute of Deity. Chalk one up for Peter. He correctly identified Jesus Christ for who He is: the Lord God Almighty.

I saw this beamed across the country during, of all things, an NFL play-off game. With four seconds left on the clock, as the place kicker lined himself up for what could have been the game-winning field goal and a trip to the Super Bowl, a television camera panned the end zone. As the ball tumbled end over end on its trajectory through the uprights, three fans unfurled a banner which read, "JESUS IS GOD." While their timing may have been questionable, their conclusion was impeccable.

Jesus Christ does indeed rule the universe. He will forever be the "KING OF KINGS AND LORD OF LORDS" (Rev. 19:16). Every living being—human, angelic, and demonic—will eventually and dramatically acknowledge this one inescapable fact.

His sovereignty is comprehensive. Consider the following:

- Jesus rules over nations. "Ask of Me, and I will make the nations your inheritance. . . . You will rule them with an iron scepter" (Ps. 2:8-9).

- Jesus rules over kings. "Jesus Christ . . . the ruler of the kings of the earth" (Rev. 1:5).

- Jesus rules over nature. "The men were amazed and asked, 'What kind of man is this? Even the winds and the waves obey Him!' " (Matt. 8:27)

- Jesus rules over diseases. "Jesus went throughout Galilee . . . healing every disease and sickness among the people" (Matt. 4:23).

- Jesus rules over life and death. "Jesus called in a loud voice, 'Lazarus, come out!' The dead man came out" (John 11:43-44).

- Jesus rules over events. " 'Go to the village ahead of you, and as you enter it, you will find a colt tied there, which no one has ever ridden.' . . . Those who were sent ahead went and found it just as He had told them" (Luke 19:30, 32).

- Jesus rules over the angels. "The Son of Man . . . will send His angels" (Mark 13:26-27).

- Jesus rules over the demons. "The demons begged Jesus, 'If you drive us out, send us into the herd of pigs' " (Matt. 8:31).

- Jesus rules over Satan. "Jesus said to him, 'Away from Me, Satan! . . . ' Then the devil left Him" (Matt. 4:10-11).

- Jesus rules over every human being. "At the name of Jesus every knee should bow . . . and every tongue confess that Jesus Christ is Lord" (Phil. 2:10-11). A certain high-school-aged middle linebacker who brazenly declared, "There's no way He's going to control my life," is in for one humongous surprise!

Contrary to much popular preaching today, we cannot *make* Jesus the Lord of our lives. He hasn't given us that option. He *is* the Lord of our lives. Nothing will ever change that. The options are reduced to but two: obedient submission resulting in God's blessing, or defiant rebellion resulting in eventual destruction (Rom. 6:16). Indeed, our children must understand that Jesus Christ is sovereign over all. He controls our lives whether we want to acknowledge this or not.

Peter understood exactly why Jesus came — "You have the words of eternal life."

What are the "words of eternal life"? Jesus said, "For My Father's will is that everyone who looks to the Son and *believes in Him* shall have eternal life" (John 6:40, emphasis mine).

Belief. Such a watered down term today. What does *belief* entail?

Pastor Sammy Tippit defines the term, not in some abstract theological fashion, but in a most practical sense as he writes from the crucible of his persecuted church in Communist Romania:

Two young people at the Communist Youth World Festival were converted instantly when they made this statement, *"Ich glaube an Jesus"* (I believe in Jesus). These two young lives were completely transformed when they made that statement. However, many people in Western Europe and the United States will say, "I believe in Jesus," but very little change, if any, is seen in their lives. What is the difference?

When those two East German youths said, "I believe in Jesus," they knew that they could lose their educational and economic opportunities in life. But they *really* believed in Jesus. They believed in His life, death, burial, and resurrection so much that they were willing to forsake all opportunities in this life in order to know Him and follow Him.

When someone in the West says, "I believe in Jesus," it can mean very little. It is usually socially and culturally acceptable to make that statement. But too often

there is no repentance, no forsaking of the old life to
follow the New-Life Giver, Jesus Christ.[1]

Jesus Christ did not come to transform our circumstances. He came to transform us. Providing us a life of ease
and comfort does not appear on Jesus' agenda. Producing *in*
us a life of Christlike character tops His list of personal priorities. As He said to the woman caught in the act of adultery,
so He says to us today, "Go now and leave your life of sin"
(John 8:11). That is why He came.

Peter understood exactly what Jesus demands— "Lord, to whom shall we go?"

That one commonly familiar title, "Lord," communicates volumes of biblical truth. The original Greek, *kurios,* denotes
both the personal respect for and the voluntary submission to
the one so addressed.

Jesus asked a most penetrating question: "Why do
you call me 'Lord, Lord,' and do not do what I say?" (Luke
6:46) Many things puzzle me about today's brand of Western-
ized Christianity. But nothing confuses me more than the
stark reality suggested by Jesus' question.

Chuck Colson, the infamous "Hatchet Man" of the
Nixon Administration, wallowed in the muck and mire of Wa-
tergate, only to arise as one of the most potent prophets of
the modern era. He writes:

Sin abounds in the midst of unprecedented religiosity.
Why? If there are so many Christians in the U.S., why
aren't we affecting our world?

I believe it's because many Christians fall into the
same trap my friend did. We treat our faith like a section
of the newspaper or an item on our "Things to Do Today" list. We file religion in our schedules between relatives and running. It's just one of the many concerns
competing for our attention.

Not that we aren't serious about it. We go to church and attend Bible studies. But we're just as serious about our jobs and physical fitness.

The typical believer, says Harry Blamires, prays sincerely about his work but never talks candidly with his non-Christian colleagues about his faith. He is only comfortable evaluating his spiritual life in a "spiritual" context. This results in a spiritual schizophrenia as the Christian bounces back and forth between the stock market and sanctification.

Such categorizing would be plausible if Christianity were nothing more than a moral code, an AA pledge, or a self-help course. But Christianity claims to be the central fact of human history: the God who created man invaded the world in the person of Jesus Christ, died, was resurrected, ascended, and lives today, sovereign over all.

If this claim is valid—if Christianity is true—then it cannot be simply a file drawer in our crowded lives. It must be the central truth from which all our behavior, relationships, and philosophy flow.[2]

Colson's last sentence brings us full circle. Jesus Christ alone rules the universe; therefore, Jesus Christ alone rules our lives—every dimension of our lives. He demands nothing less.

No one category can be severed from His sovereignty. Our goals, dreams, and ambitions must be formed and fashioned by His hand. Our family lives, social lives, entertainment, morality, values, vocabulary, work ethic, etc., must all be governed by His will. For us to tolerate anything less seriously calls into question our own identities as a Christian (Matt. 7:16, 21-23). This same standard applies equally to our children as well.

Jesus Christ alone rules the universe; therefore Jesus Christ alone rules my life.

Taking Inventory

Are You for Sale?

1. How about taking an essay exam? In your own words answer these three questions:
   a. Who is Jesus Christ?
   b. Why did He come?
   c. What does He demand?
Compare your answers to those in this chapter.

2. Now consider giving this same exam to your children. Use their responses to begin a meaningful family discussion concerning the principles laid out in this chapter.

3. Just as in Jesus' day, people today often follow Jesus for the wrong reasons. Review with your children the misguided motivations discussed in this chapter. Each, of course, applied to the crowds that followed Him in John 6. But what about today? Can you list some misguided motivations that might compel someone to follow Jesus today? Assist your children in compiling a list of the misguided motivations that might characterize a young person today.

4. Reread Sammy Tippit's contrast of Eastern versus Western Christianity. Do you agree with his observations? Why or why not? Can you pinpoint any explanation for his claim that the phrase, "I believe in Jesus" would mean so much more to a Romanian believer? Ask your children if they see any difference between Pastor Tippit's description of Romanian young people and American young people today.

5. Let's move from observation to interpretation. Lead your children to a deeper level of thinking by asking such probing questions as, "Why do you think this difference in commitment to Christ occurs?" "What have you observed that leads you to believe there is a difference?" "Do you see a difference in your own commitment to Christ compared to that of a Romanian young person?" "What should someone do to strengthen his commitment to Christ?"

6. Chuck Colson made a powerful observation. He said, "If this claim is valid—if Christianity is true—then it cannot be simply a file drawer in our crowded lives. It must be the central truth from which all our behavior, relationships, and philosophy flow." Honestly evaluate what influence, if any, Christianity has had on your behavior, relationships, and philosophy (beliefs). How about your family as a whole? Has Jesus Christ made an observable, measurable difference in these areas? Invite your children to join in the evaluation. You might be very surprised at how perceptive and insightful they can be. Please do not become defensive at anything they say. If weaknesses come to the surface, talk together about ways you can all begin to implement specific changes.

---

[1] Sammy Tippit, *Fire in Your Heart* (Chicago: Moody Press, 1987), p. 57.
[2] Charles W. Colson, *Against the Night* (Ann Arbor, Mich.: Servant Publications, 1989), pp. 163-65.

Chapter Four:
WHAT IS TRUTH?

Conviction #2 — The Bible alone is inspired by God; therefore, the Bible is absolutely true and the final authority for what I believe and how I live (John 17:17).

It could only happen in my youth group. The saga of Ida Wong will live on in infamy.

Things started out innocently enough. We decided to have a car rally. I explained the rules with painstaking clarity. "At each location you will find a clue typewritten on a 3 x 5 card. *Drive safely* ("Yeah, right! Who are you kidding, Bertolini?") to the indicated location for the next clue." Now tell me, what could be simpler than that?

As as added measure of safety, I had college students patrolling the route. If they observed any car breaking the speed limit, it would be summarily disqualified and every team member in that car would pay me a five dollar fine!

"Drivers, start your engines," I shouted over my megaphone. "To your marks, get set, go." Tires spun, exhaust fumes billowed, and off they roared.

Everything went great . . . for the first ten minutes. Then the phone rang. "Where are they?" one of my college patrol persons screamed. "We haven't seen one of them." Can you imagine trying to locate 150 high school students missing somewhere within the greater Los Angeles area?

After forty agonizing minutes, the phone rang again. "Very funny, Bertolini. Where's the next clue? We're all standing in this lady's front yard, and she can't even speak English."

"Lady, what lady?" I asked. I couldn't remember any lady on the route.

You are not going to believe what happened. The first clue read, "Exit the parking lot, then turn east and drive precisely .8 of a mile. Your next clue will be waiting for you there."

The first car out of the lot apparently had a slightly inaccurate odometer. The driver traveled .9 of a mile to a vacant lot. Naturally, twenty-nine other cars followed. The students jumped out of their cars and began scouring the lot when someone shouted, "I've got it." What he had was a wadded up, tattered and torn handwritten map to Ida Wong's house, located thirty miles away in the Hollywood Hills!

I guess that's what happens when you turn to the wrong source for directions.

Unfortunately, the overwhelming majority of young people today turn to the wrong sources for directions about life. Our society literally bombards our children with misinformation from so-called credible "experts." Indeed, it was not too long ago that a health teacher in a local high school encouraged his students to discover their sexual identity through experimentation.

"You must have the courage to face a very personal question," he told thirty-five fifteen-year-olds. "Ask yourself, 'Was I born gay?' And how do you find the answer? Why not involve yourself in one homosexual encounter? As long as you protect yourself, you've got nothing to lose. If you find it fulfilling, congratulations! You have discovered something about yourself. If not, your life will be richer for the trying."

With these kinds of voices screaming for our young peoples' attention, to what do we as parents direct our children for the answers to life's questions? In the words of Pilate, the Roman governor responsible for sentencing Jesus Christ to death, "What is truth?" (John 18:38).

In answer to Pilate's question, I would boldly declare,

The Bible alone is inspired by God; therefore, the Bible is absolutely true and the final authority for what I believe and how I live (John 17:17).

The Wonder of the Word of God

The person who discovers the limitless riches and resources of biblical truth can only respond with unbounded joy and excitement. How would a blind man react when the scales fell from his darkened eyes? Consider the sentiments of Psalm 119 as a prime example. The psalmist's wonder reverberates throughout every one of his twenty-two stanzas.

- "My soul is consumed with longing for Your laws at all times" (v. 20).

- "Your decrees are the theme of my song" (v. 54).

- "The law from Your mouth is more precious to me than thousands of pieces of silver and gold" (v. 72).

- "I have put my hope in Your word" (v. 74).

- "Oh, how I love Your law!" (v. 97)

- "I stand in awe of Your laws" (v. 120).

- "My eyes stay open through the watches of the night, that I may meditate on Your promises" (v. 148).

George Washington declared, "It is impossible to rightly govern the world without the Bible."[1] In light of our discussion, I would dare to modify his statement only slightly. "It is impossible for our children to rightly govern their lives without the Bible." We as parents must understand the four reasons why this is true.

Reason #1: The Revelation of the Bible

The Bible is the written revelation of God to us. Phrases such as *declares the LORD, the Word of God,* or their equivalents appear nearly 4,000 times within its pages! Considering the fact that there are sixty-six books in the Bible, this averages out to a staggering sixty-one claims of divine authorship per book. Do you think God is trying to tell us something?

Peter specifically detailed the concept of divine revelation when he wrote, "Concerning this salvation, the prophets, who spoke of the grace that was to come to you, searched intently and with the greatest care, trying to find out the time and circumstances to which the *Spirit of Christ in them was pointing* when He predicted the sufferings of Christ and the glories that would follow" (1 Peter 1:10-11, emphasis mine).

Ponder this point for a moment. The prophets obviously knew they were recording events that would take place perhaps centuries after they dotted their final *i*'s and crossed their final *t*'s. They diligently sought to understand the significance of what they were writing. The "Spirit of Christ" gave the revelations. The prophets recorded the information they received (1 Peter 1:12).

Did the Prophets and the Apostles understand that their words in fact constituted the written revelation of God Himself? You'd better believe it! In the first chapter of his first book, Peter seasoned eleven verses of some pretty confrontive imperatives with phrases like "It is written," "obedience to the truth," and "the living and abiding Word of God." Then, for good measure, he ended the chapter with the statement, "The Word of the Lord stands forever. *And this is the Word which was preached to you*" (1 Peter 1:25, emphasis mine). In the first chapter of his second book, Peter stated unequivocally, "Men spoke from God" (2 Peter 1:21).

Paul referrred to his reception of divine revelation as the crowning credential on his resume as an Apostle. "I want you to know, brothers, that the Gospel I preached is not something that man made up. I did not receive it from any man, nor was I taught it; rather, *I received it by revelation from Jesus Christ*" (Gal. 1:11-12, emphasis mine). He appealed to divine revelation as the sole basis for his authority in preaching. "And we also thank God continually because, when you received the Word of God, which you heard from us, you accepted it not as the word of men, *but as it actually is, the Word of God"* (1 Thes. 2:13, emphasis mine). When confronting the misuse of the gift of tongues within the Corinthian assembly, Paul ended his admonitions with the words, "Let him acknowledge that *what I am writing to you is the Lord's command"* (1 Cor. 15:37, emphasis mine).

The writer to the Hebrews continued to build the case. He pointed out that God spoke Old Testament truth through the prophets and confirmed New Testament truth through the apostles (Heb. 1:1; 2:3).

John referred to his writings as "the Word of God and the testimony of Jesus Christ" (Rev. 1:2). When we pick up our Bibles, we indeed hold the written revelation of God to us. What better legacy to pass onto our children?

Reason #2: The Inspiration of the Bible

God did not keep silent; He spoke (Heb. 1:1). Through what process, then, did the apostles and prophets record God's words to them?

Two key passages reveal and define the *inspiration* of the Word of God:

All Scripture is inspired by God (2 Tim. 3:16, NASB).

For prophecy never had its origin in the will of man, but men spoke from God as they were carried along by the Holy Spirit (2 Peter 1:21).

These thirty-one simple words contain a wealth of information worthy of our earnest consideration:

- *All Scripture.* The Greek word *graphe* as used in the 2 Timothy passage means "that which is written." It speaks of a comprehensive body of authoritative literature.

- *Inspired.* The *New International Version* correctly translates *theoneustos* as "God-breathed." Thus, the Bible is literally "that which comes out of the mouth of God — God's Word." Scripture therefore possesses divine origin and authority.

- *Carried along.* Peter chose a nautical term to express the action of the Holy Spirit in the inspiration process. The Greek word *pheromenoi* refers to a ship being carried along by the wind. As the writers recorded God's revelation, He personally bore them along, empowering and guiding them through the inspiration process. God watched over His chosen human authors, enabling them to record without error His revelation to the human race. Thus could Jesus affirm to His Father with absolute confidence, "Your Word is truth" (John 17:17).

Inspiration assures us that the Bible is complete (Rev. 22:18-19) and sufficient (Ps. 19). In the Bible, God has given us everything we need to determine what we believe and how we live (2 Peter 1:3).

The Bible alone is inspired by God; therefore, the Bible is absolutely true and the final authority for what I believe and how I live (John 17:17).

Reason #3: The Demonstration of the Bible

Talk is cheap. Anyone can write a book that claims divine authorship. I am certain that at some point in their lives every one of our children will be confronted with a most unnerving question: "How do you know the Bible is true?"

If the Bible's claims are false, we could easily prove that it isn't the Word of God. One verifiable error would suffice to completely torpedo our confidence in the credibility of the Word of God. But for nearly 2,000 years, no one has been able to document with absolute certainty one single inaccuracy within the thousands of verses in Scripture! While a comprehensive apologetic of the Bible exceeds the scope of this book, a brief sampling of the evidence would certainly be appropriate.

After sharing this information with thousands of young people over the years, including my own, I can assure you that these are the kinds of facts they love to get their hands on. I trust that your own children will feel the same.

The Amazing Unity of the Bible

The Bible was written over a period of sixteen centuries by forty different authors representing nineteen occupations. They wrote from eleven distinct geographical locations on three separate continents. They reflected the spectrum of human emotions as they employed ten different writing styles. They utilized three different languages while writing about dozens of extremely controversial subjects. Yet, the Bible reflects one consistent theme (a holy God's redemption of sinful people) with no contradictions whatsoever!

Would you like to have some fun? I've got a new party game for you. Randomly select just five people and have them write a few paragraphs about the same controversial issue. What do you suppose will be the result? Complete harmony? Total agreement? Identical theme? Not a chance. How then can you explain the fact that the biblical writers pulled off the impossible? Only one conclusion can be drawn. Men (forty of them!) carried along by the Holy Spirit indeed spoke from God (2 Peter 1:21).

The Historical and Geographical Accuracy of the Bible

How can I trust the Bible to tell me the truth about heaven and hell if it does not tell me the truth about the Hittites? Mentioned forty-seven times in the Bible, the Hittites stood for centuries as the greatest single historical embarrassment to the Bible believer. Historians gloated over the fact that not one shred of evidence could be found anywhere, apart from the Bible, to confirm that the Hittites ever existed. Until 1906. Hugo Winkler's spade uncovered the ancient capital city of the Hittite empire along with over 10,000 tablets. Historians now refer to the Hittites as one of the three most influential empires of the ancient world!

A well planned visit to your public library will reward you with volumes of archeological confirmations of biblical history. An honest scholar simply cannot deny that when all the facts are known, the Scriptures will stand as truth in everything they teach relative to history and geography.

The Scientific Accuracy of the Bible

Up until the 1400s, scientists regarded the earth as a flat disk. Isaiah wrote, in 700 B.C., that God "sits enthroned upon the circle [chug, the Hebrew word for sphere] of the Earth" (40:22). While many believed that the Earth rested on the back of a giant turtle, Job (1500 B.C.) had the audacity to declare that God "suspends the earth over nothing" (26:7). While Hippartus numbered the stars at 1,022, Ptolemy at 1,056, and Kepler at 1,055, Jeremiah referred to the "stars of the sky" as "countless" (33:22). What if the advent of the telescope had proven Kepler right and Jeremiah wrong? Our Bibles wouldn't be worth the paper they're printed on!

Solomon clearly explained the jet stream, the key to modern-day meteorology, in Ecclesiastes 1:6. William Harvey thinks he discovered the importance of the circulatory system in 1628. Wrong. Moses beat him by about 30 centuries! (Lev. 17:11) Job described the hydrological cycle (not formally discovered by science until the seventeenth century) with amazing clarity (36:27-28).

When the doctors and scientists taught that leprosy resulted from eating hot food, pepper, garlic, and the meat of diseased hogs, the solution to the plague quietly lay within the pages of the Old Testament. Following the principles of quarantine as delineated in the Book of Leviticus, the church accomplished what the then-modern day scientist could not— the methodical eradication of the disease.

The Prophetic Accuracy of the Bible

God Himself set the prophetic standard in Deuteronomy 18:20-22. His prophets must bat 1,000! Of all the religious books in print today, only the Bible stakes its credibility on the fact of fulfilled prophecy. You will find within its pages over 1,000 historically verifiable, minutely detailed predictions relative to individuals, groups of people, kings, cities, nations, and the world as a whole.

Consider the city of Tyre (Ezek. 26:1-21; 29:17-19). The prophet predicted the unthinkable and untimely demise of this impregnable seaside capital city of Phoenicia. His predictions appeared to be irrational pronouncements. He stated that Nebuchadnezzar would destroy the city, reducing the thriving metropolis to a flat rock where fishermen would dry their nets. The rubble would be cast into the sea, no plunder would be received by the conquering army, and the city would never be rebuilt.

You would do well to list the individual predictions and research for yourself the collapse of this ancient trade center. You will sit in rapt attention, spellbound by the account of Nebuchadnezzar's dismay when, after a thirteen-year siege, he discovered that the inhabitants had moved their city ½ mile off shore onto a little island. Picture Alexander the Great who, 250 years later, instructed his men to toss the rubble of the old city into the sea as he built a ½ mile long causeway out to the island city. Climb the twenty story high towers that he constructed and rolled against the fortifications. Look in amazement at some modern day pictures of this once great city. Those shadows you see are probably fishermen drying their nets on the barren rock that once was Tyre.

As you will discover, no one has rebuilt Tyre. To put this in some kind of historical context, did you realize that the city of Jerusalem has been rebuilt *seventeen times?* If someone had rebuilt Tyre just once, we could throw our Bibles away. But no one ever has. Just ask the fishermen!

Jesus Christ Himself fulfilled over 330 specific prophecies. His name, city of birth, family line, healing ministry, betrayal, method of execution, and even His resurrection were foretold with amazing clarity and accuracy.

In his book, *Science Speaks,* Peter Stoner established the probability that one man could, by chance, fulfill just eight of the 330 prophecies. Would you believe that the mathematical probability equals 1 chance in 100,000,000,000,000,000? If you covered the entire state of Texas with a pile of silver dollars two feet deep, marked one with an *X,* blindfolded a man, and let him have one pick, he would have the same chance of selecting the marked silver dollar as one man fulfilling just eight prophecies regarding Jesus Christ.[2] Anyone willing to bet against those odds?

The Honesty of the Bible

One final fact firmly places the Bible in a class all its own. The Bible tells the truth about its principle players. Have you read 2 Samuel recently? David blew it big time. The writer did not sugarcoat the scene. He did not attempt a cover-up. He did not offer any explanations or rationalizations. His no-holds-barred approach presents David for what he was—a lying, murderous adulterer. Nathan's words to his fallen king ring out loud and clear for all to hear, "You are the man!" (2 Sam. 12:7).

Noah got drunk, Abraham committed adultery and lied, Isaac became a chip off the old block and lied about his wife, Jacob extorted his brother's birthright, Moses murdered an Egyptian and buried the evidence, Aaron violated his priestly office, Samson fell because of the lustful love he had for a wretched woman, Jonah defied the revealed will of God, Hosea married a prostitute, Timothy became timid, Paul and Barnabas parted company after a heated argument, and John wanted to obliterate an entire city. It's all there for public consumption.

One further thought—the Bible is honest about us. Do you realize that with the sole exception of the Bible, no book in existence operates from the premise that man is sinful and therefore utterly helpless before God? Every other religion in the world declares that man is born inherently good and can ultimately save himself. You won't read that within the pages of Scripture. "The heart is deceitful above all things and beyond cure. Who can understand it?" (Jer. 17:9). "Surely I was sinful at birth, sinful from the time my mother conceived me" (Ps. 51:5).

Why do I believe the Bible? Because the Bible dares to tell the truth about me.

Reason #4: The Application of the Bible

The words of Solomon to his son have always been both a comfort and a challenge to me as a parent. He wrote:

> My son, if you accept my words and store up my commands within you, turning your ear to wisdom and applying your heart to understanding, and if you call out for insight and cry aloud for understanding, and if you look for it as for silver and search for it as for hidden treasure, then you will understand the fear of the LORD and find the knowledge of God. For the LORD gives wisdom, and from His mouth come knowledge and understanding. He holds victory in store for the upright, He is a shield to those whose walk is blameless, for He guards the course of the just and protects the way of His faithful ones (Prov. 2:1-8).

These words are a comfort because I know that if my children commit themselves to "living by the Book," they will never stumble off the proper path. Is that Ida Wong I hear breathing a sigh of relief? Indeed, God "guards the course of the just and protects the way of his faithful ones!"

Yet, His words provide a challenge because the responsibility for teaching biblical truth to our children lies squarely on our shoulders.

How can this be done? Deuteronomy 6:6-9 outlines a very basic three-step plan.

(1) Demonstrate in your own life a love and respect for the Word of God: "These commandments that I give you today are to be upon your hearts" (v. 6). Our children invariably mirror our attitudes and actions. Just this morning my four-year-old came into the house looking like a popsicle because she had been playing in a snow storm, in sunny Southern California no less! She pulled off her clothes, climbed into the nice hot shower and sighed, "Oh, this feels so luxurious." Now where did she come up with that expression?

I get frightened at times when I see myself reflected in my son's behavior and expressions. There is a positive side to this. What I love, my children tend to love. What I value, they value. As far as our children are concerned, our attitudes toward the Bible may well be "more caught than taught." Perhaps we should ask ourselves, "Is the Word of God impressed upon our hearts continually?"

(2) Learn to look for teachable moments: "Talk about them when you sit at home and when you walk along the road, when you lie down and when you get up" (v. 7). In other words, the routine activities of life, such as sitting at home or walking along a road, can often provide opportunities to communicate biblical truth.

So many situations in life demonstrate biblical principles, either positively or negatively. We as parents can use almost anything because it either illustrates truth or error.

Jesus was the master of this. Imagine Him stooping down, plucking a lily, and developing an entire object lesson about God's gracious provision (Matt. 6:28-34). Do you remember the time He pointed to a bird and spoke of God's faithful protection? (Matt. 10:29-30) On another occasion He made reference to a current event and from there drove home a spiritual principle (Luke 13:4).

Every time a disciple asked Jesus a question, the stage was set for a lesson. Does your child ever ask you a question? (I may as well ask you if the sun ever comes up in the morning, right?) The next time your son or daughter comes a-runnin' with a quizzical look in the eye, another teachable moment may make its glorious appearance.

(3) Place Scripture verses in prominent places around the house. "Tie them as symbols on your hands and bind them on your foreheads. Write them on the doorframes of your houses and on your gates" (vv. 8-9). Scripture verses can make wonderful plaques or posters to hang in your living room, bathroom, kitchen, children's bedrooms, etc. Something as simple as this could reap rich dividends in the lives of our children for years to come and reinforce the fact that:

> the Bible alone is inspired by God; therefore, the Bible is true and the final authority for what I believe and how I live (John 17:17).

Taking Inventory

Are You for Sale?

1. Why not make Psalm 119 the basis of your family devotions for the next few weeks? Each evening assign a section of the psalm to each family member. Allow them time to review their verses. Then instruct them to select a favorite verse, read it aloud, and explain why they selected it.

2. Make a list of some things you would never have known apart from the Bible. Have your children do the same. Share your results. Doesn't this staggering reality cause you to respect and cherish the Word of God all the more?

3. After reviewing the section titled *The Demonstration of the Bible,* have each member of your family complete this sentence: "I trust the Bible completely because . . . "

4. How much time do you spend each day reading the Bible? Does this pattern reflect a proper respect and a dependence on the Word of God?

Have you considered adopting a regular reading schedule? Why not set for yourself and your family the goal of either reading through the entire Bible once each year (four chapters per day), or the New Testament once each year (one chapter per day)? How about purchasing the Bible on cassette and listening to the Word of God while driving to work?

5. If you or your children find the Bible hard to understand, you might consider purchasing an easy to read version such as *The New International Version* or *The Living Bible*.

6. Do you own any Bible reference tools to help you better understand the Bible? A good study Bible will provide you with author, theme, and outline information. An exhaustive concordance will allow you to look up every verse in which a specific word is used. A Bible dictionary will assist you in obtaining simple definitions for complex biblical terms. Bible commentaries will help you with a verse-by-verse study. You can find a one volume commentary of the whole Bible or individual commentaries that deal with one specific book.

No doubt money will be a consideration; therefore, I recommend purchasing a good study Bible first (this will include a limited concordance), then a one volume commentary, then a dictionary, and finally an exhaustive concordance.

7. Please do not view Bible study as something you must do out of duty. See it as an adventure of discovery. By keeping your pen poised and a notebook at the ready, you will be able to record the new insights you receive as the Spirit of God guides you into the truth (John 16:13). After recording these insights in your journal, pass them on to your children, thus motivating them to dig out biblical principles for themselves.

---

[1] H.L. Willmington, *Willmington's Guide to the Bible* (Wheaton: Tyndale House Publishers, 1981), p. 796.
[2] Peter Stoner, *Science Speaks* (Chicago: Moody Press, 1963), pp. 100-107.

Chapter Five:
Is There Not a Cause?

Conviction #3—I live for the purpose of giving God glory; therefore, I must make every choice in the light of this goal (1 Corinthians 10:31).

My spare time substitute teaching at our local public high school has provided me with a bonanza of benefits. What an arrangement! At the beginning of the day the administrator hands me a key. At the end of the day, a paycheck.

What an opportunity! While in my classroom, I can answer any student initiated question. And you'd be amazed at how the students always seem to ask me just the right questions!

What a variety! I've subbed in every conceivable class you can imagine—from auto shop to zoology. On one particular occasion I found myself in the gym overseeing a co-ed sophomore P.E. class.

Sarah couldn't play volleyball due to the torn ligaments in her ankle. As she sat with me on the bleachers, I tried to engage her in an insightful conversation. I continually find myself driven to probe the adolescent mind, trying desperately to keep my finger firmly on the pulse of teenage America. I want to understand how teenagers think, what they feel, what makes them tick.

"Sarah, you can really help me," I explained. She instantly perked up. Young people today want so desperately to feel needed. "In a few weeks I will be speaking to thousands of high school students just like you in camps and conferences all across this country. I want to talk about relevant topics. If you could summarize the one question that burns the brightest in your mind or in the minds of your friends, the one issue that keeps you awake at night because you just can't figure it out, what would it be?"

For the next several minutes Sarah just stared off into a corner of the gym. She thought about my question very seriously. Finally, I saw a flicker in her eyes. "I've got a question for you," she said. "My friends and I wonder about this all the time. What's it all about?"

"What's what all about?" I asked.

"Life. What is life all about?"

Very few people understand the answer to this question. Life for most has degenerated into nothing more than a treadmill existence as they throw themselves headlong into the pursuit of an ever illusive dream—their ultimate happiness and fulfillment.

Materialistic pursuits too frequently displace proper priorities and never seem to satisfy our insatiable thirst for more. Astronomical stress levels give ample testimony to a value system that has subtly become skewed. Job dissatisfaction has reached pandemic proportions in our nation. Those who seek to find their solace in intimate, long-term relationships almost inevitably experience the disenchantment of shallow, conditional commitments.

For most people life has become agonizingly empty. In a seeming sociological contradiction, people have never had more to do, and yet, people are bored. Thus, when given half a chance, they invariably blurt out, "What's it all about?"

Reviewing our Past

I do not permit my children to utter the word *bored* in our home. I simply cannot relate to such feelings. With so many people clamoring for and sincerely needing my attention, with lessons to prepare, sermons to preach, books to read and write, places to explore, dreams to fulfill, and interests to pursue, I honestly wish that I could feel bored for a few minutes, just to know what it's like. I have often told my students, "I wish I had five lifetimes. Even that would not be enough for me to experience in life everything I would like to pursue."

A part of me recoils every time I hear a young person complain about being bored. With his entire life ahead of him, with innumerable options at his fingertips, and with the ability to set virtually any goal and throw himself wholeheartedly into its fulfillment, how can anyone honestly feel bored?

Boredom has become the root cause of a kaleidoscope of teenage conflicts. As young people live from party to party and activity to activity, their idle minds have indeed become the devil's playground. How many students turn to a bottle, powder, or pill as an antidote for a meaningless existence? How many crimes have been committed by people who simply had nothing else to do?

Young people today have lost something. In a word, they have no *cause* — nothing to live for, and certainly nothing to die for. In fact, I believe that my generation was the last in America to become galvanized by a clearly identifiable cause.

My generation lived through the Cuban Missile Crisis as our world teetered on the precipice of a nuclear holocaust. We watched in horror as our nation divided over the color of a man's skin. We mourned the senseless assassination of a popular president. Our eyes became riveted to a balcony outside a Memphis motel room as a champion for racial equality lay sprawled in a puddle of his own blood. We burned our draft cards in protest of a war we didn't understand. Berkeley became our pulpit; free speech our medium. We elected four mop-tops from Liverpool as our chief spokesmen as we sang in unison, "I Want to Hold Your Hand." Our simple lyrics called for love in a world torn by hate. We just wanted to "Give Peace a Chance."

We had a cause! We took to the streets. We marched, chanted, demonstrated, and demanded to be heard. We had no time for trivial pursuits. We were out to change the world. We knew exactly *what it was all about.*

But our cause died. Suddenly, unexpectedly, our cause evaporated into thin air. A forty-eight hour torrential deluge on a windswept grassland in upstate New York became for my generation both the culmination of a dream and the disintegration of a movement. The summer of 1969 lives on in infamy.

They came from everywhere, one-half million of my generation, to display to the world that our witch's brew of "Peace, Love, and Rock and Roll" could cure the ills of a splintered society. The bands played and the people frolicked. Love was in the air, but it was also in the sleeping bags. (The lingering question after all was said and done was: "How many babies were conceived at Woodstock?" No one will ever know.) We had finally created Utopia. Or so we thought.

The final band played. The musicians sauntered off the platform. An ominous silence, coupled with the stench of human excrement permeated the air. Trudging through the muddy quagmire, the patrons left one by one.

What became the lasting legacy of Woodstock? Cleaning crews gathered enough abandoned sleeping bags to cover every homeless person in beautiful downtown Manhattan. A two-foot-high pile of trash stretched across the vast acreage of farmland as far as the eye could see. Free love resulted in a nationwide gonorrhea epidemic. LSD, the wonder drug gateway to new vistas of human awareness, gave way to national drug addiction. Following Woodstock, the suicide rate among adolescents quadrupled.

Within one week, Woodstock promoters found themselves embroiled in a bitter legal dispute over the dispersion of the proceeds from their lucrative movie contract. Within two years two mainline performers died from self-induced drug overdoses. My generation went from the pinnacle to the pit in just over forty-eight hours. Over two decades have come and gone. Seemingly, peace still does not have a chance.

Since 1970, what cause has galvanized this generation of young people? "Save the Whales?" "Earth Day?" What are young people doing today, right now, even as you read this? Marching? Speaking? Changing the world? Hardly. Take a trip to your nearest convenience store. You'll probably find them standing in line, waiting to drop their quarters into the hottest new video game. I could just weep.

1969. What a summer! Woodstock took off like a rocket only to flame out, crash, and burn. Neil Armstrong took "one giant leap for mankind." Charles Manson went on his bloody rampage. The Miracle Mets won the World Series. But for me, another incident of monumental importance took place in the summer of 1969. I committed my life to Jesus Christ. I found a cause. I discovered *what it's all about:*

> I live for the purpose of giving God glory; therefore, I must make every choice in the light of this goal (1 Cor. 10:31).

The noble pursuits of peace and love pale into insignificance compared to the surpassing privilege of glorifying God.

Make no mistake about it. I am out to change my world, person by person, life by life. Are you? Only as we in the body of Christ collectively begin to fulfill the admonition, "So whether you eat or drink or whatever you do, do it all for the glory of God" (1 Cor. 10:31), can we begin to spawn such lasting change, especially within the lives of our children.

Defining Our Terms

"Glorifying God" qualifies as a pious platitude. But does this Christian cliché have any practical ramifications? To find out, we'll have to define our terms.

Our English word *glory* is a translation of two biblical terms—*kabod* (Hebrew) and *doxa* (Greek). From the Greek term comes the familiar "Doxology," a musical stanza which focuses our attention on "God from whom all blessings flow."

Both terms literally mean "presence, weight, or substance." Both terms can refer to men as well as to God. Among the tribal councils of Israel, an honored father of faith would stride in with great *kabod*, and the people would sense his dignity, authority, power, or weighty presence. If, within a Greek empire, a brave warrior stood to address a crowd, those gathered to hear him would feel his *doxa*, his substance as a man worthy of respect.

In reference to God, these terms reflect far more than some supposed manifestation of the supernatural. *Kabod* and *doxa* represent the weighty, substantial presence of God Himself.

Can you begin to see the significance of the phrase, "Do it all for the glory of God?" We have been given the unspeakable privilege and awesome responsibility of conducting our lives in such a way that we exhibit the presence, weight, and substance of God. In a word, our lives ought to be *distinct*.

This reality even applies to the mundane, routine activities of daily living, including eating and drinking. Let me illustrate. When I was a youth pastor, my youth group and I had a custom. Every Sunday night, after the evening service, we went to a restaurant in town for burgers and Cokes. We wanted everyone in the place to see that Christians can have fun too. So, we talked loudly and acted obnoxiously. We teased the waitresses and joked about some of the patrons. My students laughed uncontrollably when one of them placed the tip, all in pennies, under an overturned glass of water. They engaged in a variety of contests, such as attempting to balance the saltshaker on a pile of salt, or trying to throw french fries into a glass of water on an adjacent table. We drove the waitresses to distraction and left our corner of the restaurant in shambles. We achieved our goal all right. Everyone in the place knew we were there, that we were Christians, and that we were having fun. But in retrospect, I really don't believe that when we left the waitresses got together and whispered among themselves, "Wow. We have just been in the presence of young people who walk with God."

Expanding Our Definition

In order to further develop the concept of glory, consider two notable examples of the usage of our terms. The first occurs very early on, at the inception of the nation of Israel.

Moses should have been flying high. Instead, he hit rock bottom. He left the rarefied air of his face-to-face encounter with Almighty God, high atop the cloud shrouded peaks of Mt. Sinai, only to discover the debased depths to which his nation had sunk in his absence. "Go down, because your people, whom you brought up out of Egypt, have become corrupt" (Ex. 32:7).

By the time he reached the sun-parched lowlands of the northeastern Egyptian desert, the revelry was in full swing. Incensed by the scene before him, Moses shattered the two stone tablets of God's Law, symbolic of the laws the Israelites were breaking as they danced another jig around their golden calf. "And the LORD struck the people with a plague because of what they did with the calf Aaron had made" (Ex. 32:35).

From a casual reading of the Exodus account, can we even begin to imagine how Moses must have felt? At the very moment of its inception as a theocracy (a nation ruled by God Himself), Israel's foundation caved in due to the wanton behavior of its citizens. Moses' mission seemed to disintegrate right before his eyes.

In a plea of desperation Moses cried out, "Now show me your glory" (Ex. 33:18). God's answer contains some most interesting elements. "And the LORD said, 'I will cause all my goodness to pass in front of you, and I will proclaim my name, the LORD, in your presence. I will have mercy on whom I will have mercy, and I will have compassion on whom I will have compassion' " (Ex. 33:19).

Goodness, mercy, and compassion are three of God's attributes or characteristics. His name represents the totality of His being, or the sum total of His attributes. When Moses asked God to reveal His glory, God responded by parading His attributes before the eyes of His beleaguered servant. *Thus, the glory of God equals the sum total of His attributes placed on display for a watching world to see.*

God met Moses at his point of despair. At a time when nothing would satisfy Moses other than the manifested glory of God Himself, the LORD said, "There is a place near Me where you may stand on a rock. When My glory passes by, I will put you in a cleft in the rock and cover you with My hand until I have passed by" (Ex. 33:21-22).

The fulfillment finally came.

And He passed in front of Moses, proclaiming, "The LORD, the LORD, the compassionate and gracious God, slow to anger, abounding in love and faithfulness, maintaining love to thousands, and forgiving wickedness, rebellion and sin. Yet He does not leave the guilty unpunished; He punishes the children and their children for the sin of the fathers to the third and fourth generation" (Ex. 34:6-7).

How did Moses respond to this recitation of God's attributes of compassion, grace, patience, love, faithfulness, forgiveness, and wrath? "Moses bowed to the ground at once and worshiped" (v. 8). One cannot view God's attributes on public display and hope to remain the same.

A similar scene took place at the graveside of Jesus' friend. Through tear-filled eyes, Lazarus' sisters broke the news. "Lord, the one you love is sick" (John 11:3). Jesus offered comfort to the grieving women by stating, "This sickness will not end in death. No, it is for God's glory so that God's Son may be glorified through it" (v. 4).

By the time Jesus reached the grave, Lazarus had been dead for four days. The resulting dialogue between Jesus and Lazarus' sisters is most enlightening. " 'Take away the stone,' He said. 'But, Lord,' said Martha, the sister of the dead man, 'by this time there is a bad odor, for he has been there four days' " (John 11:39-40). Carefully read Jesus' reply in verse 40: "Did I not tell you that if you believed, you would see the *glory of God?*" (emphasis mine)

They removed the stone. Jesus gave the command, "Lazarus, come out!" The corpse began to stir. His lifeblood began to pulsate through his arteries. His muscles began to twitch. And his sisters watched in amazement as Lazarus walked out of his tomb alive.

The news of this miracle spread throughout the land like wildfire. God's limitless power, the attribute theologians commonly refer to as omnipotence, along with His love and compassion as He wept at the graveside, had just been placed on public display.

From these two passages then, we have learned that God's glory speaks of the presence, weight, or substance of His being. His presence is indeed most weighty or substantial because of the sum total of His attributes.

We give God glory when we place His attributes on display in our lives before a watching world. We are to carry ourselves in such a way as to reflect His presence, weight, or substance. Giving God glory must become our highest calling, greatest privilege, and most awesome responsibility. *Giving God glory enables Him to have a voice, through us, to a desperately needy and terribly confused world.* Can you even begin to conceive of a cause more vitally important than that? Giving Him glory is what it's all about.

Contrasting Our Values

Recently I engaged in a rather troubling conversation with a fairly prominent Christian businessman. After ridiculing his high-school-aged son who had abandoned the faith, he quickly blew off the rejection as "typical teenage rebellion," and changed the focus of our conversation.

"It all comes down to this," he declared, summarizing his basic philosophy of life. "I work when it rains so that I can play when it shines." He then proceeded to talk to me about his ski boat, with far greater passion, I might add, than he showed when talking about his wayward son.

Is that it? Is the purpose of life nothing more than trifling with trinkets? Perhaps I should have asked him (as well as myself) some soul searching questions: "Where are the shattered lives you are seeking to redeem? What is the message you are seeking to proclaim? What are the standards you are seeking to establish? Does your ski boat contribute to the fulfillment of these objectives? Or is it just another line item on your list of toys?"

And what about his son? Is the problem here merely "typical teenage rebellion," or is it a rejection of the contemporary hedonistic materialism that has come to characterize modern-day, Western Christianity? Could it be that this father failed to introduce his son to a faith worthy of his death, much less his life? Young people today need, want, and demand far more than our sanctified brand of recreational Christianity. No one will ever commit his life to something unworthy of his respect! What will it take to get this father to stop his playing long enough to hear the anguished cry of his searching son as he asks, "Dad, is there not a cause?"

The mother of one of my students epitomized a bogus value system. As she strolled into my office, I had to shield my eyes from the sunlight glistening off the golden earrings dangling from her earlobes. When we shook hands, I nearly cut myself on the diamonds twirling around her fingers. She defended her decision to have her son pursue a double major, youth ministry and business. "I fear that youth pastors just don't make enough money. My husband and I have worked all these years to make our children happy and comfortable. We just want to make sure that our son's standard of living won't ever have to change."

I couldn't believe it. What kind of value system is that? I did not know that a person's happiness was tied to his salary. I did not know that comfort was a part of the package.

This is war. We are embroiled in spiritual combat. We are fighting for the souls of people, the most important of whom live right under our roofs. We are rescuing men and women from eternal, conscious torment. I am training soldiers, not a bunch of spoiled little brats. We labor for the crown of righteousness (2 Tim. 4:8), not some paltry pebbles to be dangled from our earlobes.

Rethinking Our Priorities

How do we view our jobs? Our careers provide us with the platforms from which we exert our redemptive influence over the people with whom we come into contact. Our neighborhoods place us in crucibles of social interaction within which our godly messages can be proclaimed. The intimacy of our homes provides us with an environment of mutual love and support within which biblical standards can be passed from one generation to the next. I am afraid that far too few of us see life from this frame of reference.

For most, the pursuit of a career has become an end in itself, motivated by the quest for money, position, and/or power. Countless people invest forty-plus hours per week, fifty-two weeks per year, during the best years of their lives, for what? A paycheck? A title engraved in fine print on a nameplate cemented onto an office door? A personal empire built upon a foundation of blood, sweat, and tears? How many people will go to their graves with the lines of their labor etched into their faces and a two-word epitaph, etched onto their tombstone that reads, "So what?"

I refuse to allow my career to interfere with my highest calling in life; I am a husband and a father first, a college professor second. I am making career choices which appear to most as foolish. In my line of work, career advancement is tied to exposure. The more speaking I do, the more exposure I receive, resulting in greater and more significant opportunities. Nevertheless, I turn down an average of three invitations per day to speak someplace. Why? Because I am not interested, at this point in my life, in flying from conference to conference to the neglect of my family. When you understand that I receive $200 to $1,800 per engagement, the financial impact of my decisions becomes staggering.

When my daughter turns eighteen and begins to pursue her own goals and education, I will be fifty-three. God willing, I figure to have fifteen to twenty good years left. At that stage in my life, I can do all the traveling and speaking I want. But for now, I am home every night, rocking my children to sleep. Career advancement, with all of its attendant perks, has no attraction for me right now. I long to be a good husband, good father, and good professor, in that order. Anything else becomes a distraction to these high and lofty pursuits. If I can make such career choices, then so can you.

Let us never forget Jesus' promised guarantee:

> You cannot serve both God and Money. Therefore I tell you, do not worry about your life, what you will eat or drink; or about your body, what you will wear. Is not life more important than food, and the body more important than clothes?
>
> If that is how God clothes the grass of the field, which is here today and tomorrow is thrown into the fire, will He not much more clothe you, O you of little faith? So do not worry, saying, "What shall we eat?" or "What shall we drink?" or "What shall we wear?"
>
> But seek first His kingdom and His righteousness, and all these things will be given to you as well (Matt. 6:24-25, 30-31, 33).

I believe our jobs would take on a new and exhilarating dimension if we saw them as our platform from which we exert a redemptive influence on the people around us. After all, what can compare with the unspeakable privilege of placing God's attributes on display in the workplace, thereby changing our world person by person? And guess what? As an added bonus, God allows us to get paid in the process?

How do we view our neighborhoods? In many cases, neighborhoods, in the true sense of the word, have become a thing of the past. When we are not working far too many of us find ourselves dashing out the door to church services, meetings, fellowship groups, aerobic dance classes, soccer practices, choir practices, ad infinitum, ad nauseum, to the total neglect of our neighbors. While telling ourselves that these meetings are an essential part of reaching the world for Christ, I wonder how many of us are blind to some of the most needy and hurting people in the world—our own neighbors?

How do we view our families? A home should be a focal point of much redemptive activity. Within the hallowed halls of our houses, condos, or apartments, we have a golden opportunity to pass on our spiritual heritage to our children as we "bring them up in the training and instruction of the Lord" (Eph. 6:4). In addition, our homes can provide rest and refreshment to God's choice servants, a wholesome environment within which neighborhood children can play, a gathering place for friends and loved ones, food and clothing for those in need, and a source of hope and encouragement for those who hurt. Where better to place God's attributes on display before a watching world than within the intimacy of a family?

"What's it all about?" I am certain that Sarah did not fancy herself as a philosopher as she sat on the bleachers, nursing her sprained ankle. But she asked the $64,000 question. Very few people know the answer. I, along with those of my generation, spent a decade desperately searching for the answer. Sandwiched in between a moon landing and a rock concert, I finally discovered it. The last twenty-one years of my life give ample testimony to the fact that in Jesus Christ I found all that I needed. How about you?

I live for the purpose of giving God glory; therefore, I must make every choice in light of this goal" (1 Cor. 10:31).

Taking Inventory

Are You for Sale?

1. For the moment, forget what you have read in this chapter. Take an objective look at your life through the eyes of an outsider. What would he see? If he were asked to summarize an answer to the question, "What's it all about?" for you, what would he say?

2. Do you have a cause—something to live for, and if need be, something to die for? What is it? Have you committed yourself to a worthwhile pursuit? After attempting a definition, ask your spouse and your children to describe your cause. Do they see the same thing you see? Have you adequately communicated your cause to your family?

3. Without reviewing the chapter, answer this question: "What does it mean to glorify God?" Now compare your answer to the information in this chapter.

4. Make a list of God's attributes or characteristics which you can put on display in your life. Allow yourself enough time to make as complete a list as possible.

5. As a family project, you might want to select one attribute per week, making a concerted effort to build this characteristic into your lives. List specific times, places, methods, and persons to whom you and the members of your family can display each attribute. In the evening, gather your family members together and tell them of your efforts. Ask them if they have displayed any of God's attributes themselves. The success stories that you share together will serve to encourage your family members and reinforce these characteristics in their lives.

6. Have your family discuss some ideas as to how your home can serve as a redemptive influence in your neighborhood. Why not invite selected neighborhood families to your home for dinner? Rather than having your children play over at

their friends' houses, why not encourage them to bring the friends to your home? Are there needy people in your community that you and your family can assist? Be sensitive to your children's ideas. Their ideas are often some of the most creative!

Chapter Six:
THE PRIORITY OF PURITY

Conviction #4 — My body is the living temple of the Holy Spirit; therefore, I must not pollute or defile it (1 Corinthians 6:15-20).

LeAnn longed to hear the words, "Daddy's little girl." But the words never seemed to come.

They used to. In fact, LeAnn's dad said them often as his favorite expression when referring to his daughter. Until one day when everything seemed to change.

LeAnn was home alone and taking a shower. Two teenage boys decided to break in and steal whatever they could for some extra spending money. After all, they had a rather expensive drug habit to support. They did not realize that somebody was home.

LeAnn wrapped herself in a towel and walked from the bathroom to her bedroom to get dressed. Without a moment's hesitation, one of the guys grabbed the towel from her grasp while the other threw her to the floor. I am sure that you can imagine the rest.

As suddenly as the attack began, it ended. The boys ran out of the house, leaving LeAnn in a state of emotional and physical shock. Her life began to unravel on the floor of her own bedroom.

Two months later, LeAnn continued to suffer from chronic depression and never-ending nightmares. Finally, not knowing what else to do, her parents placed her under the care of a "Christian psychologist." After several weeks of therapy, LeAnn finally mustered enough courage to ask her counselor the question that burned brightest in her mind: "Dr. _____, what do you think of me?"

He responded, "Well, LeAnn, what did you expect would happen when you parade yourself around like that in front of two boys while wearing nothing more than a towel?" His answer pushed her over the edge.

LeAnn tried one more desperate act of survival. She got on a church bus bound for Hume Lake Christian Camps. As she sat in the back of the bus alone with her thoughts, she silently prayed, "Dear God, please, I beg you, send someone who can tell me what You think of me." Nobody knew that if she got a response similar to that of her counselor, she would carry out the suicide she had planned out in minute detail.

As she and I sat next to the lake, I had the distinct privilege of introducing LeAnn to the liberating truth of Deuteronomy 22:26, "She [the rape victim] has committed no sin."

"LeAnn," I explained, "no one can take your purity away. You are the victim of a horrible crime, true, but nothing more. You are as pure as newly fallen snow."

As her eyes exploded with emotion, she asked, "Would you please explain that to my dad. Ever since I got raped, he will not hug me, and he doesn't call me 'Daddy's little girl' anymore."

I defy you to find any term in the English language that carries more of an electrically charged punch than the word *rape*. No horror, no personal tragedy, can begin to compare. The magnificent panorama of our nation's heritage has been indelibly marred by the black blot of rape that daily plagues our streets and back alleys. For this reason I find myself taking a monumental risk by raising this issue.

While I have never experienced this trauma personally, I have spoken to dozens who have. We must never trivialize nor underestimate the emotional and physical scars inflicted by such an atrocity. Words cannot describe the utter violation of an innocent human being as he or she is forced to lie helpless while the aggressor perpetrates whatever vile act he may choose. No wonder God declares in reference to rape, "The man who has done this shall die" (Deut. 22:25).

My intent in writing this chapter is not to focus upon the subject of rape. But then again, in an offhanded way, maybe it is.

Webster's defines rape as, "an outrageous violation," and "an act or instance of despoiling a person by force." According to this definition, one victim of rape, I dare say, remains anonymous. He will never appear on Donahue. Oprah has yet to interview him. Once Geraldo gets hold of this one, you can bet another primetime special will come roaring down the pike.

Later in this chapter we will consider the true identity of *this* rape victim. But first, how about a little tidbit of information? Do you have any idea which segment of our population commits the rape of this victim with greater frequency than any other? Christian young people. That's right. Our children are a part of a high risk group when it comes to perpetrating this particular crime. Furthermore, you and I as parents are not exempt from possibly doing the same. You'll understand what I mean as you keep reading, all the while remembering our conviction:

My body is the living temple of the Holy Spirit; therefore, I must not pollute or defile it (1 Cor. 6:15-20).

Let's begin by setting the stage.

A Corinthian Catastrophe

Corinth, a key city in ancient Greece, serves as a fitting backdrop as our saga unfolds. Rebuilt by Julius Caesar as a Roman colony in 46 B.C., Corinth eventually grew and prospered, becoming the capital of the province of Achaia. Strategically located on a narrow isthmus between the Aegean and

Adriatic Seas, Corinth blossomed into a major commercial center containing, among other things, two vital seaports. In Paul's day, the city boasted a population of 700,000 people.

Corinthian carnality has been well-documented. The Corinthians cavorted about, throwing themselves pell-mell into whatever sensual stimulation struck their fancy. Any semblance of morality was out; "Anything goes" defined their value system. "If it feels good, do it" summarized their ethics. The All-American Corinthian held tenaciously to one, and only one, nonnegotiable conviction: "There are absolutely no absolutes."

The family unit had all but disintegrated, falling prey to a steady diet of immorality, adultery, homosexuality, and a skyrocketing divorce rate. A clue to contemporary Corinthian culture can be found tucked away in the middle of Paul's first letter to the struggling church he himself founded in the midst of this cesspool society:

> Do you not know that the wicked will not inherit the kingdom of God? Do not be deceived: Neither the sexually immoral nor idolaters nor adulterers nor male prostitutes nor homosexual offenders nor thieves nor the greedy nor drunkards nor slanderers nor swindlers will inherit the kingdom of God. And that is *what some of you were.* But you were washed, you were sanctified, you were justified in the name of the Lord Jesus Christ and by the *Spirit of our God* (1 Cor. 6:9-11, emphasis mine).

Following that thumbnail description of life on the streets in beautiful downtown Corinth (or Los Angeles, San Francisco, New York, Chicago, etc.), Paul authored the key passage that is the basis for the conviction of this chapter:

> My body is the living temple of the Holy Spirit; therefore, I must not pollute nor defile it (1 Cor. 6:15-20).

In stark contrast to the prevailing moral anarchy of his day,

Paul called upon Christian Corinthians to live a morally blameless life.

God has clearly placed a priority on personal purity. Paul linked the importance of this imperative to the person of the Holy Spirit and the revolutionary concept of our bodies as His temple.

In order for us to teach this conviction effectively to our children, two questions must be considered. First, "Who is the Holy Spirit?" And second, "What is the significance of the temple?"

The Mysterious Member of the Trinity

During his third missionary journey, Paul asked a group of Ephesian believers a very provocative question. "Did you receive the Holy Spirit when you believed?" Their answer shocked him. "No, we have not even heard that there is a Holy Spirit" (Acts 19:2).

Most of us have one up on them. We have at least *heard* of the Holy Spirit. But how many believers today adequately *understand* exactly who He is?

As we sift through the volumes of information the Bible reveals about the Holy Spirit, three facts must be considered in order to properly understand Paul's admonition to us in 1 Corinthians 6:15-20.

(1) The Deity of the Holy Spirit. Scripture describes the Holy Spirit as a coequal with God the Father and God the Son. When we talk about the Holy Spirit, we are talking about Almighty God Himself (Acts 5:3-4).

(2) The Personality of the Holy Spirit. The Holy Spirit must never be thought of as a *something,* but rather as a *someone.* He is not an impersonal force floating throughout the universe. The Holy Spirit possesses every attribute of personality, including a mind (Rom. 8:27), a will (1 Cor. 12:11), and emotions (Eph. 4:30).

(3) The Indwelling of the Holy Spirit. Paul wrote, "Don't you know that . . . God's Spirit lives in you?" (1 Cor.

3:16). Can you even begin to fathom the meaning of these words? The Holy Spirit goes where we go, sees what we see, and hears what we hear. And believe it or not, as a permanent resident within our bodies, the Holy Spirit becomes a participant (willingly or unwillingly) in whatever we do, quite possibly experiencing great grief in the process (Eph. 4:30). Hence, we have an awesome responsibility that our children must understand:

My body is the living temple of the Holy Spirit; therefore, I must not pollute nor defile it (1 Cor. 6:15-20).

A Building Not Made with Hands

Our bodies are referred to repeatedly as His "temple." The significance of this word cannot be overstated.

The temple basically consisted of three sections: the "Outer Court," to which the people had access; the "Holy Place," to which the priests had access; and "The Holy of Holies," to which no one had access, with one exception. Only one man, the high priest, on only the Day of Atonement, could walk behind the veil separating the holy place from the holy of holies. And he could do so in only one way, by first offering for himself a blood sacrifice. Why? Because God manifested Himself in the holy of holies. His glory flamed and flashed behind that veil. No one except the high priest could walk into the presence of Almighty God and live.

Immediately after Jesus died, before the earth shook and rocks split, "the curtain of the temple was torn in two from top to bottom" (Matt. 27:52). God gave us a dramatic object lesson. The veil was torn, not from the bottom to the top by a human hand, but from the top to the bottom by a divine hand, illustrating for all to see that God no longer dwells in buildings made with hands!

He now lives in us. "Do you not know that your body is a temple of the Holy Spirit, who is in you, whom you have received from God?" (1 Cor. 6:19) His Shekinah glory now flashes and flames within us. At least it should. God no longer manifests Himself through radiant light as in the Temple of old. Today He manifests Himself through our transformed lives. Remember our last chapter? We live to reflect His glory as we place His attributes on public display. And so do our children! Thus, our commitment to the present conviction must be unwavering:

My body is the living temple of the Holy Spirit; therefore, I must not pollute or defile it (1 Cor. 6:15-20).

A Solution to Pollution

Reread 1 Corinthians 6:9-11. Pollution and defilement can take place in a myriad of ways. You would do well to launch yourself into a personal study of each of the terms listed in this passage. I should like to develop two of them. I am appalled that today, in many of our evangelical churches, these two acts of blatant compromise are generally regarded as acceptable behavior.

An example of pollution: "Drunkards."

Today, the most commonly used drug in America is alcohol, the drug of choice among most teenagers and their parents. Every day in this country Americans consume 1.2 million gallons of hard liquor, producing a devastating effect on some 56 million families. Did you know that in this country one out of seven people who drink alcohol in any form will become a chronic alcoholic?

The battle is on for our youth. By the time he is eighteen, the average student will have seen over 100,000 beer commercials. The result? Since 1966, the number of high school students who are intoxicated at least once a month has more than doubled. By their senior year, nine out of ten high school students will have begun their mad dash down the dead-end street of drinking. An estimated 3.3 million drinkers ages fourteen to seventeen show signs that they may develop serious alcohol-related problems, possibly including alcohol-related highway deaths, the number one killer of fifteen to twenty-four year olds.

On the average, a person's first experience with alcohol now occurs at age twelve, usually involving beer or wine coolers. Can you guess the most common reason given for beginning to drink? Mom and Dad's example.[1]

Needless to say, I take a very strong stand against drinking. Ten years ago, in churches across our nation, I was given standing ovations for my conviction. Today, in those same churches, I am often crucified for suggesting that Christians must not drink. The criticism often comes as fast and furiously from the preachers in the pulpits as it does from the people in the pews.

"You're too legalistic," someone will say. "Jesus Himself turned water into wine," another will add. Someone else will insist, "Paul commanded Timothy to drink." And then there is the ubiquitous rationalization: "The Bible nowhere says it's a sin to drink as long as we don't get drunk."

Yes, Jesus did turn water into "wine." Yes, Paul did command Timothy to "use a little wine because of your stomach and your frequent illnesses" (1 Tim. 5:23). Yes, Paul did say not to "get drunk on wine."

However, our English Bibles use two distinct words relative to alcoholic beverages. "Wine" refers to a heavily diluted beverage. This fermented grape juice beverage served as both a water purifier and medicine. Yes, a person could get drunk from drinking "wine." But in most cases, he would have to consume it by the gallon.

What we call wine, beer, or wine coolers today the Bible refers to as "strong drink." "Strong drink" is expressly forbidden in Scripture:

> Wine is a mocker and beer [*strong drink* in both the KJV and NASB] a brawler; whoever is led astray by them is not wise (Prov. 20:1).

But all of that aside, we must not drink because we cannot run the risk of someone else, especially our children, taking a drink as a result of our examples. We are attempting to set a godly standard in a world where virtually no standards exist. We cannot allow anything, especially a little glass of wine with our dinner, to hinder us in fulfilling our life's purpose.

I routinely ask teenage audiences, "If you knew that I drank alcohol, how many of you would no longer respect anything I teach?" Without exception, one out of three students raises his hand. No can of beer is worth that.

> My body is the living temple of the Holy Spirit; therefore, I must not pollute nor defile it (1 Cor. 6:15-20).

An example of defilement: "Sexually immoral."

Over the years, I have heard more camp talks on the subject of teenage sexuality than I can count. Without exception, the speakers base their messages on the lingering consequences a person might face as a result of moral indiscretions. Statistics abound as to the number of sexually transmitted diseases, the possibilities of pregnancy, the horrors of abortion, etc. These kinds of warnings certainly have their place. I applaud the efforts of those who have put their reputations on the line by taking a most unpopular stand.

There exists, however, another vitally important motivation for maintaining personal purity. Biblically, the strongest statement concerning sexual immorality appears in 1 Corinthians 6: "Flee from sexual immorality" (v. 18). In supporting his point, the Apostle Paul nowhere appeals to statistics and warnings about diseases. He builds his argument on a much more significant foundation.

> Flee from sexual immorality. All other sins a man commits are outside his body, but he who sins sexually sins against his own body. Do you not know that your body is

a temple of the Holy Spirit, who is in you, whom you have received from God? You are not your own; you were bought at a price. Therefore honor God with your body (1 Cor. 6:18-20).

Sex is God's wedding present to the human race. When my dear wife and I got married, it was exciting to come home from our honeymoon to a house full of wedding gifts. Yet, much to our dismay, we received an unbelievable number of duplicates: five Crockpots, seven sets of towels, three toasters, etc. (Don't tell anyone, but we kept the best for ourselves and gave the duplicates away as wedding presents to our friends!)

On our wedding night, however, we received one gift that no one duplicated. As a supreme expression of His love toward us, God gave us our most treasured wedding present: the marriage bed (Heb. 13:4). God personally designed the bliss and ecstasy of the marriage bed for our enjoyment throughout our married lives. How He must grieve when His unique gift becomes soiled and defiled through its misuse outside of marriage.

Paul offers a most sobering argument. When two believers in Christ who are not married engage in a sexual union, they are in effect prostituting the living temple of the Holy Spirit. Am I overstating the case? I think not. "Do you not know that your bodies are members of Christ Himself? Shall I then take the members of Christ and *unite them with a prostitute?* Never!" (1 Cor. 6:15, emphasis mine)

My body is the living temple of the Holy Spirit; therefore, I must not pollute nor defile it (1 Cor. 6:15-20).

Coming Full Circle

Rape has become a scourge in our society. No atrocity can begin to eclipse the degradation brought by this horrendous violation of a human being. Forcing someone against his or her will into an immoral act which so horribly tramples his dignity is nothing short of unthinkable and unconscionable. I know. Last summer I talked at length to "Daddy's little girl" who was raped in her own home.

The Holy Spirit lives within your body and within mine. As God, He is spotlessly holy. As a person, He feels emotions deeply. As the indweller of our bodies as His temple, He goes where we go, sees what we see, hears what we hear, and participates willingly or unwillingly in whatever we do.

By engaging in vile acts of pollution (by what we place into our bodies) or defilement (by what we do with our bodies), are we not forcing the Holy Spirit against His will into situations which horribly trample His dignity? Are we not committing "an outrageous violation of His holiness? Are we not "despoiling a Person by force?" Are we not in effect *raping* the Holy Spirit? Keep in mind that I am not making a statement but rather asking a question, one that deserves our careful consideration. And are we not thereby causing Him immeasurable grief? Indeed, we must teach our children to honor the Holy Spirit with their bodies no matter what personal sacrifices of their sensual pleasures such effort may demand (1 Cor. 6:20).

My body is the living temple of the Holy Spirit; therefore, I must not pollute nor defile it (1 Cor. 6:15-20).

Taking Inventory

Are You for Sale?

1. Since Corinthian culture so dominates the contents of 1 Corinthians, why not lead your family in a background study of the book? Try to determine exactly what was going on in the streets of Corinth. Ask yourselves, what kind of moral setting were the believers in that struggling church facing every day? Ask your children if they can pinpoint any similarities to our own culture.

2. The Holy Spirit is holy. Expand on that thought. As a family, discuss what holiness really means in terms of the character of God. According to 1 Peter 1:14-16, how should this fact affect our lives?

3. We are commanded not to grieve the Holy Spirit (Eph. 4:30). Has anyone in your family ever been grieved? Discuss together the sensations that person felt. Point out that the Holy Spirit feels the same way, even more deeply, when we grieve Him. Ask the members of your family how this principle applies to their lives.

4. The indwelling of the Holy Spirit is a most fascinating study. Have your family study Acts 2. What exactly happened there? Next, check out Romans 8. Write down every reference to the Holy Spirit in that chapter. If your Bible has cross-references in the margin, look up the related verses. Discuss together how His indwelling should influence your moral decisions.

5. First Corinthians 6:9-11 summarizes the categories of compromise that pollute and defile the temple of the Holy Spirit. Lead your family in a discussion concerning the meaning of these key terms.

6. Are you guilty of polluting or defiling the Holy Spirit in your own life? If so, what steps must you now take to correct this most serious situation? Do you need to ask your children to forgive you for the poor example that you have set?

---

[1] Stephen Arterburn and Jim Burns, *Drug Proof Your Kids* (Pomona, Calif.: Focus on the Family Publishing, 1989), p. 12.

Chapter Seven:
IT'S ALL IN THE FAMILY

*Conviction #5 — My marriage vows constitute
an unconditional commitment to God first
and to my spouse second; therefore, I must honor
this commitment for as long as we both shall live
(Matthew 19:6).*

Bobby would not establish eye contact with me. When I met him at the junior high winter camp, I could tell he felt deeply troubled about something. I tried to proceed gently as I probed and prodded him to open up. But he refused to respond and would not look me in the eye.

At one point in our rather one-sided conversation, I just happened to mention in an offhanded way, "It must have been tough for your mom to say good-bye to you yesterday. I'll just bet she misses you a lot, doesn't she?" No sooner were the words out of my mouth than the dam holding back his tears broke.

"I don't understand what happened," he told me. "We used to be so happy together. My dad was an engineer and we had lots of money and everything. We used to do things together all the time. But then it just stopped.

"My dad stopped coming home at night. My mom and him started arguing all the time. He stopped doing things with us. And now he's married to somebody else. I wish I knew what happened. Whenever I ask my mom, she just starts crying and gets mad at me. She cries all the time now.

"Do you remember last night when you asked everyone, 'What's the one thing in life that you want?' Well, I thought about that all night in my cabin. Do you know what's the one thing in life that I want? I just want my mom to be happy again."

As I sat in the chapel talking with Bobby, I witnessed another impersonal statistic become a living, breathing flesh-and-blood reality right before my eyes. I did not know what to say. I could only throw my arms around him and listen to him cry.

Hanging on the Horns

Confession is good for the soul. At the outset of this most controversial chapter, I find myself in need of making a confession to you.

I continually find myself hanging on the horns of a dilemma. This particular predicament rears its ugly head almost every time I preach, teach, or write. I have yet to find the answer to my problem, even though I have pursued its solution relentlessly.

I will phrase my plight in the form of a question. "How can I persuade people to commit themselves to a specific biblical conviction without causing undue pain to those who have already violated it?" When I uphold a biblical standard, I often devastate an entire segment of my audience for whom my message comes too late. Yet, when I emphasize God's compassion, mercy, and cleansing, I run the risk of creating the perception that failure is no big deal; God will merely forgive and forget, allowing the offending party to live happily ever after. So what do I do?

As is true with most dilemmas, the answer cannot be found in either extreme. Balance is the order of the day. Much to my dismay, however, I must confess to you that I rarely achieve the proper balance.

The topic of this chapter presents me with a dilemma. So often, the subject of marriage and divorce finds peoples' nerve endings rolling all over the floor. One simply cannot deal with this issue without stepping on someone s toes. The emotional scars left in the wake of a broken marriage often throb for a lifetime. Well-intentioned discussions concerning the sanctity of marriage too often rip the wounds open again, causing the victims of divorce to cringe with every word.

Believe me, I have no desire to inflict such pain on anyone. I have experienced firsthand the agony of divorce. My father moved out just as I hit the ripe old age of sixteen. My dear mother had to fend for herself. My two younger sisters and I were forced to adjust to an entirely new and extremely difficult lifestyle. We all still feel the effects of a marriage gone sour. Yes, I understand.

Tragically, in any given local church, the divorce rate represented within the pews has too often reached staggering proportions. In spite of this fact, I do not focus on anyone's past. I seek to condemn no one. This chapter has not been written with the motive of bringing judgment on anyone regarding any decisions made in the months or years gone by. Such haranguings would benefit no one. I am content to leave the past in the past. My concern lies solely with the future—the future of our children, our churches, and ultimately our nation.

For us as parents, the time has come to work together to salvage the next generation, especially their future marriages. In this chapter, we shall take a bold look at the meaning and application of Jesus' words to His pharisaical critics, "So they are no longer two, but one. Therefore what God has joined together, let men not separate" (Matt. 19:6).

Midterm Exam

"Is it lawful for a man to divorce his wife for any and every reason?" (Matt. 19:3). With this question, the Pharisees, the self-righteous religious leaders of Jesus' day, opened a veritable Pandora's Box. This question is still being asked today, even (or should I say especially) within Christian circles.

Confusion abounds as to the theological and legal implications of marriage and divorce. Often, Christians cite so-called "irreconcilable differences" to justify the pandemic incidence of divorce and remarriage that plagues the body of Christ today. The unfortunate reality cannot be denied; too many Christians today are divorcing their spouses "for any and every reason."

Our present sad state of affairs is actually nothing new. When the Pharisees asked Jesus their question, they were making a feeble attempt to trap Him into taking an unpopular stand on a most provocative subject. You will note that they questioned Him in front of "large crowds" (Matt. 19:2). They sought to "test" Him (Matt. 19:3). In large measure today, the church of Jesus Christ is being tested in front of the large crowds of the watching world on this very issue. The corporate credibility of the church hangs in the balance.

Did Jesus pass this midterm exam? Does His answer have any lingering ramifications for Christians today? Indeed, "Is it lawful (biblically acceptable) for a man to divorce his wife for any and every reason?" For the sake of ourselves, our children, and the watching world, we must come to grips with His answer.

Laying the Foundation

In articulating His response, Jesus appealed to the first book in the Bible:

Haven't you read . . . that at the beginning the Creator "made them male and female," and said, "For this reason a man will leave his father and mother and be united to his wife, and the two will become one flesh?" So they are no longer two, but one. Therefore what God has joined together, let man not separate (Matt. 19:4-6).

The situation in the Garden to which Jesus refers lays the foundation for a proper understanding of the God-ordained institution of marriage. A phrase-by-phrase consideration of Jesus' answer will highlight and amplify the beauty and sanctity of the marriage relationship. In blatant contrast to the current confusion, the biblical ethic concerning marriage and divorce is extremely easy for us and our children to understand.

"Haven't you read?"

By prefacing His statement with these three words, Jesus underscored the authority of the Old Testament. God has already spoken on this subject. His words are not mere fodder, intended to fuel ethical discussions or theological debates. He responded by stating absolute truth for our personal application and obedience.

"At the beginning."

This pattern, established by God, transcends time and culture.

"The Creator made them male and female."

God created exactly *one* woman for the *one* man. When God declared that "It is not good for the man to be alone," He followed up His pronouncement with His proposed solution. "I will make a helper [singular, not plural] suitable for him" (Gen. 2:18).

"For this reason."

God's creative acts did not come to a completion with the creation of Adam. God created one additional entity. He created a family. By dividing the human race into two genders, God decreed that the family unit would serve as the most basic building block of all future civilizations.

"A man will leave his father and mother."

Marriage produces a new family which takes precedence over every other human relationship, including old family ties. The family unit must be protected and preserved at all costs.

"And be united to his wife [singular], and the two will become one flesh. So they are no longer two, but one."

During a wedding ceremony, the bride and groom stand before a man of God in the presence of God Himself, His holy angels, and His people, as they pledge their lives to one another for as long as they both shall live. God now sees the husband and his wife as one. This lifelong union of body, soul, and spirit is divisible only by death (Rom. 7:2).

"Therefore what God has joined together, let man not separate."

God never included divorce in His plan for the human race. He hates it (Mal. 2:16), forbids it (Matt. 19:6), and desires to abolish it for any and every reason (Matt. 5:31-32). The time for us to begin teaching this conviction to our children is now.

> My marriage vows constitute an unconditional commitment to God first and to my spouse second; therefore, I must honor this commitment for as long as we both shall live.

A Picture Worth 1,000 Words

A casual perusal of the New Testament presents the reader with ample testimony to the sanctity of marriage within the heart of God, a sanctity which I long to communicate to my children. For example:

- Jesus wove the marriage customs of His day into a story to illustrate our anticipation of His return.

> But while they were on their way to buy the oil, the bridegroom arrived. The virgins who were ready went in with him to the wedding banquet. And the door was shut. . . . Therefore keep watch, because you do not know the day or the hour (Matt. 25:10, 13).

- Paul chose the metaphor of marriage to illustrate the relationship of Jesus Christ with His church:

Husbands, love your wives, just as Christ loved the church and gave himself up for her to make her holy, cleansing her by the washing with water through the word, and to present her to himself as a radiant church, without stain or wrinkle or any other blemish, but holy and blameless (Eph. 5:25-27).

- John uses a similar comparison to communicate Christ's commitment to, as well as the awesome radiance of, the redeemed city, our eternal dwelling place, the New Jerusalem:

One of the seven angels ... said to me, "Come, I will show you the bride, the wife of the Lamb." And he carried me away in the Spirit to a mountain great and high, and showed me the Holy City, Jerusalem (Rev. 21:9-10).

Each of these three examples establishes our eternal security as believers in Jesus Christ. As His bride, we can *confidently* await His coming for us as a loving and faithful bridegroom. We can *confidently* long for that day in which He will present us holy and blameless. We can *confidently* expect to dwell securely in His presence as citizens of the breathtakingly beautiful city of God. We are *confident* because in each example, God fulfills His commitment to us *unconditionally*. Jesus Christ will never file for a divorce!

Divorce Destroys

Divorce simply does not constitute a viable option for God's people. Too much hangs in the balance. Divorce destroys the very metaphor God uses most often to underscore the security of the relationship we enjoy with Him.

Divorce destroys the credibility of Christianity in the eyes of the children involved. A Jesus who is unable to keep a mom and dad together within the intimacy of a family is a Jesus unworthy of the children's respect and devotion. Countless young people have rejected Christ as teenagers because the divorce of their Christian parents caused the credibility of Christianity to collapse right before their eyes.

Divorce destroys the credibility of Christianity in the eyes of a watching world. The plea, "Beloved, let us love one another" rings pretty hollow when a Christian husband and wife cannot love each other. If Jesus' words are true, "All men will know that you are My disciples if you love one another" (John 13:35), then divorce can only cause the unsaved to conclude that Christian discipleship is meaningless.

Divorce simply is not an option for God's people. We must pass on this biblical conviction to our children:

My marriage vows constitute an unconditional commitment to God first and to my spouse second; therefore, I must honor this commitment for as long as we both shall live.

Yeah, But . . .

Are there not some notable exceptions to the rule? The Pharisees certainly thought so. "Why then . . . did Moses command that a man give his wife a certificate of divorce and send her away?" (Matt. 19:7).

You talk about a loaded question. Do you see that troublesome word *command?* The Pharisees sought to imply that divorce, in some bizarre way, constituted obedience to the will of God! Don't roll your eyes too quickly. I've had more than one Christian man express to me that God led him to divorce one wife in order to marry another.

The Pharisees, searching for an exception to God's law, referred to a supposed command from Moses. I diligently searched the five books of Moses, Genesis through Deuteronomy, trying to find this command. Finally, after an exhaustive study, I found it, in Deuteronomy 24. Admittedly, this discussion gets a bit technical. Yet, in the interests of completeness for the sake of our children, let me show you exactly what Moses did say.

If a man marries a woman who becomes displeasing to him because he finds something *indecent* about her, and he writes her a certificate of divorce, gives it to her and sends her from his house, and if after she leaves his house she becomes the wife of another man and her second husband dislikes her and writes her a certificate of divorce, gives it to her and sends her from his house, or if he dies, then her first husband, who divorced her, is not allowed to marry her again after she has been defiled. That would be detestable in the eyes of the LORD. Do not bring sin upon the land the LORD your God is giving you as an inheritance (Deut. 24:1-4, emphasis mine).

Moses did not command that a man divorce his wife.

He only commanded that once a divorce and subsequent remarriage had taken place, the wife must never, under any circumstances, return to her ex-husband.

Moses did permit divorce, but only in the case of "indecency," something morally unclean, dirty, vile, and shameful.

The Pharisees made a gargantuan leap from the intent of Moses' statement in Deuteronomy 24:1-4 to their question of Matthew 19:7. Jesus addressed this fact when He said:

Moses permitted you to divorce your wives because your hearts were hard. But it was not this way from the beginning. I tell you that anyone who divorces his wife, except for marital unfaithfulness, and marries another woman commits adultery (Matt. 19:8-9).

Many people have referred to these verses as the so-called "exception clause." A close examination of Jesus' words will bring crystal-clear clarity to the entire marriage-divorce-remarriage issue.

Fact: Moses did permit divorce.

Fact: Moses permitted divorce *only* in cases of un-clean, dirty, vile, shameful, immoral indulgences, extreme enough to warrant the designation "indecent."

Fact: Moses permitted divorce *only* because of the hardness of men's hearts. As a concession to the "innocent party," when hardhearted, non-repentant, ongoing indecency took place, a divorce would be *allowed*, never *commanded*.

Fact: Even under these conditions, God did not origi-nally include divorce in His plan—"But it was not this way from the beginning" (Matt. 19:8). From the beginning God's standard has consistently been no divorce.

Fact: Jesus allows divorce under the same circum-stances as Moses does. The phrase "marital unfaithfulness" is a translation of the Greek term, *porneia*, from which we get our English word *pornography*. Thus, by choosing this vividly descriptive word, our Lord permitted divorce only in the case of hardhearted, nonrepentant, ongoing "pornographic" or "in-decent" behavior.

Fact: Divorce for any other reason is illegitimate and results in adultery for those who remarry.

Permitted, but Never Commanded

Moses and Jesus had good reasons for allowing divorce in the case of hard-hearted, nonrepentant, ongoing immorality. Al-low me to suggest a few:

- When a person commits an immoral act, he violates the sanctity of his marriage relationship (Heb. 13:4).

- In marriage "the two become one flesh." Immorality violates *this* union and creates a union with another (1 Cor. 6:16).

- Sexual immorality is to the body what spiritual prostitution is to the soul (Ezek. 16:15, 20).

- Under the Old Testament economy sexual immorality carried the death penalty (Deut. 22:22). We do not live under Old Testament Law. Today, God's grace allows an adulterer to live. Must the "innocent party" suffer because God's grace allows the immoral husband or wife to live? Certainly not.

The Bible does allow one other legitimate reason for divorce:

> But if the unbeliever leaves, let him do so. A believing man or woman is not bound in such circumstances (1 Cor. 7:15).

God permits divorce in the case of hard-hearted, non-repentant, ongoing immorality. God also permits divorce when an unbelieving spouse chooses to leave his or her believing partner. In such instances, the Christian husband or wife is not bound by the marriage vow, and is thus free to remarry.

"But You Don't Understand. I'm So Unhappy."

Apart from the exception mentioned above, the Christian must never initiate the divorce. And for a very good reason:

> If any brother has a wife who is not a believer and she is willing to live with him, he must not divorce her. And if a woman has a husband who is not a believer and he is willing to live with her, she must not divorce him. For

the unbelieving husband has been sanctified through his wife, and the unbelieving wife has been sanctified through her believing husband. Otherwise your children would be unclean, but as it is, they are holy (1 Cor. 7:12-14).

Now we come to the crux of the issue. Many Christians today feel "trapped" in unhappy marriages. Immorality may not be a part of the equation. Yet, due to those infernal "irreconcilable differences," people may be miserable nonetheless. Is there no way out for them?

We all know of Christian friends or relatives who do indeed consider themselves trapped. They long for a way out at all costs. They regard as most repulsive even the slightest hint that their marriage should be preserved.

Whenever we encounter such scenarios, we feel torn emotionally, do we not? We naturally feel sorry for our loved ones who find themselves in such desperate situations. We don't like to see people suffer. We desire to greet them with the news of some pain-relieving options. At times, however, there simply are no options. "If any brother has a wife who is not a believer and she is willing to live with him, *he must not divorce her*. And if a woman has a husband who is not a believer and he is willing to live with her, *she must not divorce him*" (1 Cor. 7:13-14, emphasis mine).

But why not? Is God some kind of heavenly ogre who delights in our misery? No Way!

There is much more at stake than our personal happiness. Please consider the fact that divorce destroys the redemptive influence that a believer can have in his own home (1 Peter 3:1-7). That is precisely what Paul meant when he referred to an unbelieving husband or wife being "sanctified" through the believing spouse.

The word *sanctified* refers to an act of God which sets someone apart for His own plans and purposes. Through the godly influence of a believing husband or wife, the unbelieving spouse and children will experience the collateral blessings and attendant benefits of living with a Christian.

When a Christian initiates a divorce from an unbeliever, he or she robs God of the opportunity to use his or her life as a redemptive influence in the home. The point should be obvious. A person's passion for reaching the lost must include his personal passion for reaching the lost under his own roof. Divorce destroys a believer's opportunity/to fulfill that passion.

One Last Thought

Tragically, over the years, I have encountered situations in which obedience to 1 Corinthians 7:12-14 would result in physical and emotional damage to the believing wife and/or her children. Does God intend for a Christian woman to expose herself or her children to the physical abuses of an out-of-control husband? Fortunately, God addresses this specific issue in 1 Corinthians 7:10-11:

> To the married I give this command (not I, but the Lord): A wife must not separate from her husband. But if she does, she must remain unmarried or else be reconciled to her husband. And a husband must not divorce his wife.

In such extreme cases of physical or emotional abuse, God does permit *separation,* but not *divorce.*

Putting It All Together

So here I am again, hanging on the horns of a dilemma. I know that some of you reading this chapter have already violated the truths related here. My words have ripped open your wounds and stung your heart. Believe me, I sought to cause no unnecessary pain to anyone. The scars I bear because of my own parents' divorce run deep. Please view me as one who sympathetically understands.

Yet, I find myself weary of picking up the shattered

pieces of young lives reeling and rocking in the wake of the devastation caused by the breakup of their own families. "When will it stop?" I cry out in desperation, especially after crying with young people like Bobby. Somehow, some way, we've got to help the next generation return to the sanctity of the marriage vow. Our children must be taught now the truths contained within this biblical conviction:

My marriage vows constitute an unconditional commitment to God first and to my spouse second; therefore, I must honor this commitment for as long as we both shall live (Matt. 19:6).

And so I take a monumental risk by daring to declare God's truth concerning an explosive issue that now rages out of control. May the words of our Lord Jesus Christ bring the church back to an even keel as far as our children's future marriages are concerned.

So they are no longer two, but one. Therefore, what God has joined together, let man not separate (Matt. 19:6).

Taking Inventory

Are You for Sale?

1. The testimony of Hosea has stood for centuries as a model of how to handle a most unpleasant marriage. As a family read together his story, writing down the difficulties he faced, his responses, and the blessings of God that resulted. What does Hosea's unconditional commitment to his wife reveal about God's unconditional commitment to His people?

2. To pass on this conviction concerning marriage to our children, I would suggest the following.
    If yours is a happy marriage, illustrate to your children God's blessing on your home as a result of your

honoring this conviction. Be transparent about the fact that in every marriage, the husband and wife must work out their differences and struggles. Nobody ever said that marriage would be easy. Yet, the effort has certainly been worth it.

If your children have experienced your failed marriage, talk openly about the causes of the problems and the scars that have resulted in your life. Children can learn as effectively from "corrected failure" as they can from a more positive example. Stress their need to take their own marriage vows very seriously as they cautiously choose their future spouse.

3. Do you know of anyone who feels trapped in a difficult marriage? Can you offer comfort by trying to paint the much bigger picture of becoming a redemptive influence in the home? Carefully read 1 Peter 3:1-7. List each of the principles mentioned there. Offer constructive input as to how your friends can maintain a godly example in their own homes.

4. Let us never forget our own responsibilities to bear one another's burdens. Are any of your friends suffering through a divorce? Do your children have friends who are growing up in a broken home? If so, discuss together ways in which you can offer yourself as an understanding support interested in rebuilding broken lives.

5. Given the importance of marriage, now would be a good time to help your sons and daughters set some responsible guidelines as to whom they will date, develop standards concerning the physical aspect of dating, and clarify their own nonnegotiables regarding a future mate. So many tragic situations can be averted if proper preparation has been made even before a person begins dating. I believe that we as parents are supremely responsible for preparing our children for the pressures they will face in dating, engagement, and marriage.

Chapter Eight:
The Sanctity of Life

*Conviction #6—Man is created in the image of God;
therefore, all human life is sacred
(Psalm 139:13-16).*

As Hilary walked off the plane, everyone's heart seemed to melt. Disappointment swept through the crowd. Why? I did not know. But I would find out.

Anticipation had been running high. My youth group was about to receive its first foreign exchange student. The girls had shopping sprees planned, and the guys talked incessantly about "the cute little European girl" who was coming. We all gathered at the airport and anxiously awaited her arrival. But as Hilary entered the terminal and waved her arms to greet us, something was obviously wrong with my youth group.

The next several months were agonizing for me to watch. The girls canceled their plans to introduce Hilary to the shopping malls. None of my guys asked her on a date. I heard no more talk about "the cute little European girl." In fact, everyone seemed to abandon her.

Hilary grew despondent and homesick. She had planned on visiting in America for one year, but twelve months now seemed an eternity to her. She felt all alone, with no friends, no family, nobody to talk to. Whenever she walked by a group of young people, the conversation invariably seemed to drop to a whisper. I even thought I heard people snicker at her behind her back. As the leader of my youth group, I felt ashamed. Hilary decided that she just didn't like America very much.

Things finally reached a boiling point. Hilary was going to join our group for her very first camping experience. No one would sit with her on the bus. When we arrived at the camp, no one wanted to stay in her cabin. No one ate with her in the dining hall. No one asked her to join the recreation. I couldn't take it anymore.

I pulled some of my key student leaders aside and asked them point blank, "Why are you treating Hilary like a misfit?" No one would give me a straight answer. In a fit of desperation, I cornered one of my most trusted guys. "Look, Tom," I told him. "You and I have never had any hidden agendas. Let's not start now. What is the deal with Hilary? I have got to know."

He hemmed and hawed, stammered and stuttered. Finally, he dropped his eyes as if ashamed, and in a hushed tone admitted the problem to me. I stood there dumbfounded, refusing to believe what I was now hearing. "The problem with Hilary is this," Tom confessed. "She doesn't shave under her arms."

Needless to say, my youth group and I were headed for a showdown. I am of the conviction that prejudice in any form, for any reason, must not be tolerated.

Fearfully and Wonderfully Made

Apparently some members of my youth group had forgotten something. Scripture declares:

> For You created my inmost being; You knit me together in my mother's womb. I praise You because I am fearfully and wonderfully made; Your works are wonderful, I know that full well. My frame was not hidden from You when I was made in the secret place. When I was woven together in the depths of the earth, Your eyes saw my

unformed body. All the days ordained for me were written in Your book before one of them came to be (Ps. 139:13-16).

An evolutionist would have us believe that we humans are mere animals, the products of a *natural* process rather than the objects of a *supernatural* act of creation. The Bible clearly declares that within the natural process of procreation, God has intimately involved Himself in the formation of every human being. And He makes no mistakes! This fact gives every one of us personal worth. We are of infinite value, whether we choose to shave under our arms or not!

You and I have been "knit together," "made," and "woven together." David understood this "full well." Do we? Have we consistently passed on to our children this conviction regarding the sanctity of all human life?

Genesis 1:26-27 adds definition to the Psalmist's declarations:

Then God said, "Let Us make man in Our image, in Our likeness, and let them rule over the fish of the sea and the birds of the air, over the livestock, over all the earth, and over all the creatures that move along the ground." So God created man in His own image, in the image of God He created him; male and female He created them.

We parents must understand that evolutionary teaching has robbed the youth of our day of their dignity as human beings, reducing them to mere animals. And with that, respect for human life has been thrown to the winds. These words from Genesis ought to restore our children's dignity to its rightful place. Their proper self-respect, as well as their respect for the sanctity of all human life, hinges upon a proper understanding of "the image of God;" therefore, we must consider the question, "What does 'in His own image' mean?

Genesis 5:1-3 gives us the proper interpretation of this phrase:

When God created man, He made him *in the likeness of
God.* He created them male and female and blessed
them. And when they were created, He called them
"man." When Adam had lived 130 years, he had a son *in
his own likeness, in his own image;* and he named him
Seth (emphasis mine).

The word *likeness* used both in reference to God and
to Adam clearly reveals the significance of the phrase, "the
image of God." Seth was a mirror image of his father Adam.
The characteristics intrinsic to Adam's nature were also true
of his son. In the same way, we are all mirror images of God.
As human beings we share in common many of the characteristics of God. This is not to suggest, as some have, that we
are little gods. Let me make this point perfectly clear. To say
that we possess some of God's characteristics is *not* to claim
divinity in any sense of the word. God has said, "I am the
LORD; that is My name! I will not give My glory to another"
(Isa. 42:8).

Pretend for a moment that you did not have a Bible.
What could you determine about God by simply observing
people?

- People possess intelligence. Since intelligence cannot
  come from non-intelligence, God must have an intel-
  lect equal to, if not greater than, the combined intel-
  lects of 5.2 billion people. We call this *omniscience.*

- Men can communicate with each other. God must
  therefore possess the ability to communicate. We call
  this *divine revelation.*

- Men have an inborn sense of good versus evil. God
  must Himself possess morality. We call this *holiness.*

- Men have the capacity to love one another. Love cannot originate from a nonloving source. The Bible refers to God's unlimited and unconditional love as
  agape.

- Men punish evildoers. So does God. We call this *justice.*

- Men often care for the less fortunate. God Himself is the author of *compassion.*

- Men seethe in anger over injustice. So does God. The Bible calls this His *wrath.*

- Men often forgive those who have hurt or offended them. God performed the ultimate act of forgiveness when He saved us by His *grace.*

Do you get the point? God has granted to us a measure of His own characteristics. Thus, you and I are, to a degree, mirrored reflections of Him. We have been created "in His image." We human beings possess a most valuable quality, something which the animal world can never know. As people, made in His image, we possess *dignity.*

The Indignity of It All

We possess dignity. What a concept! How desperately our children need to understand this. *Webster's* defines dignity as "the quality or state of being worthy, honored, or esteemed." As the capstone of God's creation, men and women made in His image should be esteemed as such.

Yes, His image in us has become tarnished because of the Fall. The Bible declares that the human heart is "deceitful above all things and beyond cure. Who can understand it?" (Jer. 17:9). So, due to our depravity, we live in total dependence upon Jesus' saving work on the Cross. Yes, we live within a delicate tension—total depravity balanced with God-given dignity.

You'd never know it from the way we humans often treat one another. Even the hearts of the redeemed, often exhibit a critical, judgmental, prejudicial spirit, illustrated with our words and our actions. Have we as parents communicated such an attitude to our children?

Prejudice in any form is an insidious and odious disease of the heart. None of us is immune. Even though we would all decry the horrors of such a thing, this attitude can pulsate through our arteries without us even recognizing its presence. Until we are forced to take a personal inventory, that is. The remainder of this chapter is dedicated to just such an examination.

For the sake of our discussion, I have isolated three common forms of prejudice. As we develop these examples, join me in evaluating our own heart regarding this sensitive issue, all the while keeping in mind:

Man is created in the image of God; therefore, all human life is sacred (Ps. 139:13-16).

Racial Prejudice

What is your attitude toward those of other races? Please do not be too quick to answer. As you consider the following questions, keep in mind that I join you in asking them of myself.

- Do we ever stereotype an individual based on the color of his skin or the shape of his eyes?

- Do we find ourselves unwilling to associate with or befriend another due to his nationality?

- Do we ever engage in humor at another's expense, especially in a race-related way, such as ethnic jokes?

- Do we dehumanize another by referring to him by color or race, rather than by his name?

- How would we react if our children seriously dated someone of another race? Would we forbid our children to marry interracially?

- Do we blame the condition of the economy or the tensions in the world on certain races of people?

Some people may be shocked to learn that Jesus Christ was not a white man. He came from the one part of our world that touches Europe, Asia, and Africa. No race, no ethnic group can claim a monopoly on Jesus. Have we forgotten that Christianity is *not* a "white man's religion."

When we kneel at the cross of Christ, we cannot, we dare not, come up with a color in our eyes, except one. The only color we should see at the cross is red, the red of the blood that He shed for "the sins of the *whole world*" (1 John 2:2, emphasis mine). The blood that spilled from His wounds onto the ground represented every single race on Planet Earth. May we never forget the words of the four living creatures and the twenty-four elders who will sing throughout eternity,

> You are worthy to take the scroll and to open its seals, because You were slain, and with Your blood You purchased men for God *from every tribe and language and people and nation.* You have made them to be a kingdom and priests to serve our God, and they will reign on the earth (Rev. 5:9-10, emphasis mine).

Do you begin to get a feel for the subtlety of this issue? Let me give you one example that just popped into my mind. A friend of mine was recently discussing his zeal for missions with a group of parents and their children. As they prepared to pray for the Middle East, an obvious compassion concerning the Arab peoples emerged. When my friend mentioned his concern for those of Jewish descent, however, he was taken aback by a rather severe reaction.

"Hey, they had their chance and they blew it," one person declared. "Don't forget, Christ first offered His kingdom to the Jews. And what did they do?"

"They killed Him," another added.

A third parent chipped in, "That's right. And they deserve all the suffering they have received."

They then bowed their heads and prayed passionately

for the worshipers of Allah. All the while, their children sat at their sides, all ears tuned into their dialogue. Did these parents understand that they were subtly molding their children's values regarding racial equality? I think not. Do they really hold to the conviction of this chapter?

Man is created in the image of God; therefore, all human life is sacred (Ps. 139:13-16).

Prejudice against the Elderly

Our culture places a premium on youthfulness. It's not polite to ask another his or her age, as if aging is something we should deny. Corporate American often invents creative inducements to encourage an early retirement, thus clearing the way for those with youthful ambition to claw their way to the top. Rest homes are doing a banner business these days as we pay others to tend to the needs of our own. Do our families and our churches value the presence of the elderly, or do we merely tolerate them as we invite them to name our ministries in their wills?

God has much to say concerning the elderly, and especially widows. James records for us the following clear command:

Religion that God our Father accepts as pure and faultless is this: to look after orphans and widows in their distress and to keep oneself from being polluted by the world (James 1:27).

When Isaiah pronounced God's displeasure with Judah, he began by pleading the widows' plight:

Learn to do right! Seek justice, encourage the oppressed. Defend the cause of the fatherless, plead the case of the widow.
Your rulers are rebels, companions of thieves; they all

love bribes and chase after gifts. They do not defend the cause of the fatherless; the widow's case does not come before them (Isa. 1:17, 23).

In fact, in 1 Timothy 5, God devotes fourteen verses to the proper treatment of widows within the context of the local church. Among other things, Paul wrote:

Give proper recognition to those widows who are really in need. . . . No widow may be put on the list of widows unless she is over sixty, has been faithful to her husband, and is well-known for her good deeds, such as bringing up children, showing hospitality, washing the feet of the saints, helping those in trouble and devoting herself to all kinds of good deeds (1 Tim. 5:3, 9).

How many of our churches take these verses literally? Does your church have a "list" of widows it chooses to support? Are the widows in our churches honored members due to the godly examples they have set for the younger members to follow? Or have they been neglected, or worse, relegated to a second-class position?

Paul also instructed Timothy to teach his people their own responsibilities to the elderly, specifically the widows in their own families:

Give the people these instructions, too, so that no one may be open to blame. If anyone does not provide for his relatives, and especially for his immediate family, he has denied the faith and is worse than an unbeliever. . . . If any woman who is a believer has widows in her family, she should help them and not let the church be burdened with them, so that the church can help those widows who are really in need (1 Tim. 5:7-8, 16).

The elderly have a secure place within the heart of God. They should within the hearts of our families as well.

Why? They bring to our children an indispensable quality—
the wisdom that results from walking with God for years.
They can tell priceless stories of God's faithfulness over
time. They can teach measureless lessons, carefully prepared
within the crucible of their own lives. The examples they can
set, based on years of quiet consistency and enduring faithfulness, is of inestimable significance.

I do not want my children sitting at the feet of some
thirty-year-old Christian rock musician who is, more often
than not, more enamored with his own abilities than he is
with the person of a Holy God. I want my children to sit at
the feet of spiritual fathers and mothers who "have known
Him who is from the beginning" (1 John 2:12, 14), men and
women who have come to know God in the depths of His
eternal attributes by walking with Him for years.

Prejudice against the Handicapped

The word *handicapped* refers to someone who has "a disad-
vantage that makes achievement unusually difficult," so says
Webster's. But achievement in what realm? The physical
world of the athlete, with which we seemed to be consumed,
is narrow indeed. By this definition, we all possess a handicap
of one kind or another.

Our society has duped us into believing that certain
attributes, such as the ability to walk, are necessary in order
for one to enjoy a quality life. Such a view is far too limited.

The Bible nowhere supports such a view. In fact, God
has declared that His power "is made perfect in weakness"
(2 Cor. 12:9).

Human experience nowhere supports such a view.
Some of the happiest, most fulfilled people you and I know
possess what some would call a physical or a mental handicap. I defy any sociologist anywhere in the world to discover
a correlation between fulfillment in life and a person's physical ability, academic aptitude, or financial wherewithal.

Our discussions within our families must never support this view. According to Psalm 139:13-16, God has created every human being with the potential for achievement.

Once again, we turn to the little book of James in order to find God's perspective on this issue.

My brothers, as believers in our glorious Lord Jesus Christ, don't show favoritism. Suppose a man comes into your meeting wearing a gold ring and fine clothes, and a poor man in shabby clothes also comes in. If you show special attention to the man wearing fine clothes and say, "Here's a good seat for you," but say to the poor man, "You stand there," or, "Sit on the floor by my feet," have you not discriminated among yourselves and become judges with evil thoughts? (James 2:1-4).

While this passage clearly places the context of partiality within the framework of the rich versus the poor, the underlying principle of the passage still relates directly to our discussion. Do we base a person's value or worth on his physical, mental, or financial abilities or inabilities? If so, we violate the very intent of James' admonition.

As is so often the case with James, he tends to restate or reapply words already spoken by his Lord. Consider Jesus' words in Matthew 25:

Then the King will say to those on His right, "Come, you who are blessed by My Father; take your inheritance, the kingdom prepared for you since the creation of the world. For I was hungry and you gave Me something to eat, I was thirsty and you gave Me something to drink, I was a stranger and you invited Me in, I needed clothes and you clothed Me, I was sick and you looked after Me, I was in prison and you came to visit Me."

Then the righteous will answer Him, "Lord, when did we see You hungry and feed You, or thirsty and give You something to drink? When did we see You a stranger and invite You in, or needing clothes and clothe You?

When did we see You sick or in prison and go to visit
You?"
The King will reply, "I tell you the truth, whatever
you did for one of the least of these brothers of mine,
you did for Me" (Matt. 25:34-40).

By referring to "the least of these brothers of mine,"
Jesus indicated that a true measure of our spiritual condition
is our willingness to serve those who cannot, in any tangible
way, give anything back in return. Have we become partial in
our responses to "the handicapped," or do we view every
person, regardless of his physical, mental, or financial condition, as someone created by God with the potential for
achievement, and thus someone we must willingly serve?

Do we live in violation of these principles? Consider
the following illustrations.

Recently, a student came to me with tears in her eyes
and bitterness in her heart. She expressed to me her compassion for the homeless and her desire to work in a homeless
shelter after she graduates from college. So far so good. Then
her eyes flamed as she told me about her Christian parents,
both of whom are in the ministry.

"Whenever we drive downtown and see homeless
people on the street," she lamented, "my mom always has to
make some crack about them. Why can't she understand that
not everyone can be as fortunate as she is?" A careless,
offhanded comment so often communicates volumes to our
children about the prejudices of our hearts. Fortunately, this
girl knew enough to reject her mother's attitude, even
though she felt wounded by the memory.

Last month I had the privilege of speaking at a fund
raising banquet for a most worthwhile Christian organization.
Thirty minutes before I was to speak, the master of ceremo-
nies approached me and asked, "Can you tell me everything
that you've done for the last five years so that I will know
how to introduce you."

After giving him a thumbnail sketch of my recent

involvements, I later thought to myself, *Why am I invariably introduced in this way? Why is it never enough just to say, "We are privileged tonight to have as our speaker a man who walks with God?"* In our contemporary Christianity, "walking with God" just isn't enough. People want to know where I've spoken, what I've written, and if I've been to the former Soviet Union yet. At times, quite frankly, I get so tired of playing "the game." Our personal worth must never be assessed by what we do, but rather by what we are.

We are all capable, at certain times and in certain ways, of becoming prejudiced people. We may say that all human life is sacred, but all human life is not necessarily sacred to us. This must change. As parents, we dare not cheapen anyone's life in the eyes of our children through our words, actions, or attitudes. If we desire to reflect a Christ who loves the whole world (John 3:16), including a girl named Hilary, we must be models of love ourselves. For as Jesus said, "A new command I give you: Love one another. As I have loved you, so you must love one another. By this, all men will know that you are My disciples if you love one another" (John 13:34-35).
Let us never forget that:

man is created in the image of God; therefore, all human life is sacred (Ps. 139:13-16).

Taking Inventory

Are You for Sale?

1. Discuss together both the definition and the significance of the phrase, "Created in God's image." How should this reality impact your view of yourself and others?

2. Reread the questions listed under the category, "Racial Prejudice." Are any of these true of you? In what ways, if any, do you or the members of your family reveal a preju-

diced attitude toward others? Can you think of constructive ways in which you can show an unconditional love toward them now?

3. How would you describe your attitude toward the elderly? Respect? Resentment? Indifference? How do your children perceive your attitude toward the elderly based on any comments you have made in the home? Does anything need to change? If so, how?

4. Are you guilty of showing partiality toward anyone, based on a physical, mental, or monetary "handicap"? If so, can you identify the reasons? What steps will you need to take in order to change your attitude?

5. The three types of prejudice discussed in this chapter certainly do not constitute an exhaustive list. As a family, discuss this question: "Do we harbor any prejudicial spirit in our own hearts?" If you decide that you do not, go out to dinner and celebrate. If you determine that prejudice does exist in some form, go out to dinner and discuss ways in which you can make some measurable changes.

6. Prejudice can strike like a viper. Resolve together as a family that you will now hold one another accountable in terms of inappropriate words or attitudes communicated within your home.

Chapter Nine:
TAKE ME TO YOUR LEADER

Conviction #7—God has placed me under authority
for my protection and direction; therefore, I must obey those
in authority over me, with a joyful attitude, until I am
required to disobey the Word of God
(1 Samuel 15:23).

Diana, one of my most faithful volunteer staff members, rushed up to me just moments before we began our high school Bible study one evening. "Look," she exclaimed, as she flashed a shimmering diamond before my eyes. "Rob just asked me to marry him, and I said 'Yes!' And we wanted to tell you before we told anyone else in the youth group!" What a thrill! If ever there was a "marriage made in heaven" this was it!

"Hey," I said, "why not announce your engagement to the whole youth group tonight?" And so they did. A hundred students went berserk and every person in the room felt ecstatic. Rob and Diana even got a standing ovation. After everyone calmed down, I asked them all to turn to Ephesians 6:1-3, and I launched into my topic for the evening—parental authority.

The Bible study ended and everyone went home, except Diana and Rob. When they approached me, I could see that Diana had been crying and Rob looked terribly troubled.

"What's wrong?" I asked. "You two ought to go out and celebrate."

"I don't think we can anymore," Diana answered. "You see, we have a problem. When we told my parents about the engagement, they weren't exactly excited. My dad doesn't really care. He likes Rob and everything. He feels like its my life and I can do what I want. My mom's the problem. She likes Rob too. She just doesn't think we're ready.

"See, I kind of knew this might happen, because my mom feels like she got married too young. Since I'm their only child, they've always worried about me. I'm twenty-three years old, and they still treat me as if I'm thirteen.

"Well anyways, we just figured that since we're Christians and they aren't, and since we've prayed about this and everything, well, we figured it was God's will for us to get married. But after your lesson tonight, we're just not sure. Dewey, what do you think we should do?"

I felt as if someone had just punched me in the stomach. These two precious people, whom I love so much, had shared with me the greatest joy of their lives. And barely two hours later I killed it.

How would you have answered Diana's question? Should they move forward with their plans? Should they break their engagement? Should they put their plans on hold indefinitely? If you would like to know what I told them, keep reading. You'll find my response buried somewhere in the middle of this chapter.

Respect for authority has hit an all-time low. Governmental officials, employers, teachers, and parents have become high-level targets. Our "Me First" mentality has propelled those who espouse anarchy from the depths of the despised to the heights of a hero. We really should not be surprised. Paul said it would be this way:

But mark this: There will be terrible times in the last days. People will be lovers of themselves, lovers of money, boastful, proud, abusive, disobedient to their parents, ungrateful, unholy, without love, unforgiving, slanderous, without self-control, brutal, not lovers of the

good, treacherous, rash, conceited, lovers of pleasure
rather than lovers of God—having a form of godliness
but denying its power (2 Tim. 3:1-5).

Paul declared these words as a prophecy of future
events. For us, they come as a declaration of a pitiful, present
reality.

Did you notice that right smack dab in the middle of
this rather inauspicious list of attributes, the phrase "disobedient to their parents" appears? In contrast to the descriptions that immediately precede and follow it, this phrase may
not sound so wild and wicked. Words like *brutal* and *slanderous* sound far worse, do they not?

Look a little deeper. "Disobedience" communicates
an attitude of wholesale rebellion. "To their parents" speaks
of an authority meltdown within the most intimate of human
relationships—the family. Indeed, "disobedience to their parents" strikes at the very heart of the problem. Every despica-
ble description in 2 Timothy 3:1-5 flows out of a disintegrated
authority structure. How must we as parents protect our own
families from such a sorry state of affairs?

Warnings from a Raven

God has never been One who lacked for words. He is the
master at painting a mental masterpiece. Some of His verbal
brushstrokes evoke pleasant, heartwarming responses within
readers, while others provoke sheer terror. Proverbs 30:17
serves as one such example for our children to heed: "The
eye that mocks a father, that scorns obedience to a mother,
will be pecked out by the ravens of the valley, will be eaten
by the vultures."

"That's so gross," one high school student resounded
as I read aloud those words. The imagery is most vivid. Ravens, I am told, are scavengers. When they light on a carcass,
in order to insure that death has overtaken the beast, they
will invariably peck at the eyes. If an eye does not twitch, the

ravens can be assured that death has overtaken their prey. Vultures are also scavenger birds. They fly high in the sky, their eyes zeroed in on the goings on far below them. When they observe the ravens preparing for their banquet, the vultures swoop down, chasing the ravens away. Then they settle in to complete the task the ravens began.

The application to our discussion is most sobering: attitudes of rebellion in the hearts of our children constitute their first steps toward spiritual death and decay.

Samuel drew the boundary lines even tighter. "For rebellion is like the sin of divination, and arrogance like the evil of idolatry" (1 Sam. 15:23). What is the "sin of divination?" It is willingly exposing our lives to the realm and power of Satan. Rebellion equals just such an act.

The reason for such strong words can be found in Isaiah 14:13-14. When Lucifer fell and became Satan, five times he uttered the two deadly words, "I will." No longer did this "anointed cherub" (Ez. 28:14) find himself content as an angel of special significance. He coveted a higher position. He longed to crown himself as the "Most High" (Isa. 14:14). His *modus operandi?* An attitude of rebellion.

An Obligation to Obey

Scripture says much concerning our attitudes toward those in authority over us, including our government (Rom. 13:1-7), our employers (Col. 3:22-25), the leaders of our churches (Heb. 13:17), and our spouse (Eph. 5:21-33). As parents, we would do well to *teach* these principles to our children.

As parents, we would also do well to *model* these principles to our children. I had to learn this one the hard way. My son became my teacher and my car became my classroom. As we were driving one day, David leaned over to me and asked, "Hey Dad, how come you only buckle your seat belt when a policeman drives by? Aren't you supposed to wear one all the time?"

"Come on, David," I responded. "The government

has no right to tell me what I can or cannot do in the privacy of my own car. The Seat Belt Law is a stupid law. Besides, I hate wearing a seat belt." He just looked at me and said, "But it's the law, Dad." I now buckle my seat belt. Have you ever faced any similar circumstances? Indeed,

> God has placed me under authority for my protection and direction; therefore, I must obey those in authority over me, with a joyful attitude, until I am required to disobey the Word of God (1 Sam. 15:23).

In order for us to teach and model this conviction to our children, we must consider together seven important questions.

1. What is God's purpose in placing us under authority?

The Bible presents a two-pronged answer—our protection and direction.

The protection aspect can be clearly seen in Ephesians 6:1-3:

> Children, obey your parents in the Lord, for this is right. "Honor your father and mother"—which is the first commandment with a promise—"that it may go well with you and that you may enjoy long life on the earth."

Certainly Paul did not intend to create the perception that obedience will guarantee anyone a long life. Death is no respecter of persons. However, all things being equal, an obedient individual will experience a longer and more tranquil life than a rebel.

From the moment of the Fall of Man, God initiated the principle of authority. "Your desire will be for your husband, and he will rule over you," God said to Eve (Gen. 3:16). The entrance of sin into the world necessitated a need for the protection that divinely appointed authority can bring.

I believe that this protection comes in two realms. God uses those in authority over us to protect us from harmful situations He knows we cannot handle, as well as from harmful temptations. As a youth pastor I have seen both of these illustrated in rather dramatic fashion.

During her freshman year in college, Christy maintained a weekly ritual. She visited her friend Lisa's apartment every Friday night. On one particular Friday evening, something seemed different — Christy's mother begged her not to go. Christy became upset as she reminded her mother that she was now of age. Her mother pleaded with her, but to no avail. Christy stormed out of the front door, slamming it as she went. Five hours later a madman jumped out of a bush, held a knife to her throat, and threatened to kill her.

I am not suggesting for a minute that every time we disobey someone in authority, we will get attacked. Nor am I suggesting that obedient people are exempted from personal tragedy. However, I am suggesting that in this case God used Christy's mom to warn her concerning this traumatic event. Since the word *children* in Ephesians 6:1 has no inherent age connotation (the word refers to anyone living under the parents' roof, dependent on their provision), Christy certainly should have honored and obeyed her mother.

Jim got bored sitting around the house at night. Even though he would not graduate from high school for another two months, he hung around several college-aged friends. They went into Westwood every night; he had to stay home. So, creative guy that he was, Jim stuffed his bed with blankets, creating the appearance that he was sound asleep, and then he promptly climbed out his bedroom window.

As his youth pastor, I could tell that Jim had changed. I cornered him in his living room one evening and demanded a full explanation. He lowered his head and began to recount story after story of overwhelming temptations that he never expected to face. Today he will tell you that our little living room encounter saved his life. He now realizes that God used the voice of his parents, and later his youth pastor, to protect him from harmful temptations that God knew he could not handle. God always provides a way of escape (1 Cor. 10:13). That way of escape often comes through those whom God places in authority over us.

Protection is only half the story. I believe that God uses those in authority to provide direction for our lives. Nehemiah (Neh. 2) and Daniel (Dan. 1) certainly understood this principle. So did Diana. Do you remember her from our opening story?

The exciting news of her engagement to Rob spread through our church like wildfire. As the students in my youth group returned home after Bible study and shared with their parents the exciting news, Rob, Diana, and I were huddled in my office considering the question, "Dewey, what do you think we should do?"

I sat silently and wondered to myself if I had taught them correctly. If ever an exception to the rule existed, Rob and Diana certainly qualified, didn't they?

Why would God block this engagement? I asked myself. *Any mother would give her right arm to have a son-in-law like Rob,* I thought. *What could possibly be accomplished by frustrating their plans?* I hashed and rehashed this question in my mind.

Finally, I cleared my throat and said, "Rob, Diana, there are times in everyone's life when he or she must make a decision with the brain, rather than the heart. For you, this is one of those times. Diana, if your mother feels this strongly about the engagement, then I must conclude that it's either the wrong time, the wrong person, or both. I would recommend that the two of you yield to the wishes of Diana's mother and ask God to confirm His will for your lives through her." This moment was so difficult for me that I choked on every word I spoke.

Diana gave back her ring, and they informed her par-

ents that they would not get married until they had their full
support. The next week, they stood in front of my youth
group once again and explained to the young people the reasons for their decision. One hundred students sat in stunned
silence.

Several agonizing months went by. Then, finally, out
of the blue, Diana's mother said to her daughter, "You have
shown such maturity in these past few months that your
father and I have decided that you can get married." I think
the entire city must have heard Diana scream into the
mouthpiece of the phone, "Rob, we can get married!"

I had the privilege of officiating the ceremony. I have
never witnessed nor been a part of a more special occasion.
The radiant testimonies of these two young people were so
compelling that five of their guests later informed the happy
couple that they had prayed to receive Christ during the
wedding. Rob told me that due to some unexpected setbacks
in his job, "It would have been a financial disaster for us if we
had gotten married when we had originally planned."

Does Scripture support the idea that God expresses
His will through those in authority? One little statement in
the Book of Nehemiah should jump off the page at us. "It
pleased the king to send me; so I set a time" (2:6). After
Nehemiah had prayed for God's favor in the eyes of his
"boss" (1:11), God confirmed Nehemiah's desire to rebuild
Jerusalem's wall as His will indeed. Nehemiah then determined the proper timing through the authority of the king
whom he served.

2. How does God want us to respond to those in author-ity over us?

The answer can be found in Ephesians 6:1-2, "Children obey
your parents in the Lord, for this is right. 'Honor your father
and mother.' " Let's define our terms. *Obey* simply means to
do what we are told. *Honor* means to treat someone with the
same respect with which we would treat Jesus Christ if He

were here. *Obey* refers to an action, while *honor* refers to an attitude.

Within the framework of an employer-employee relationship, Colossians 3:23 reinforces this ethic of obedience and honor. "Whatever you do, work at it with all your heart, as working for the Lord, not for men."

Likewise, Romans 13:2 states, "Consequently, he who rebels against the authority is rebelling against what God has instituted, and those who do so will bring judgment on themselves." Thus, even with regard to the government, our response must be one of honor and obedience.

While these verses offer some obvious implications for those *under* authority, they also imply a warning for those who *are* the authority. In a sense, we parents represent God within our homes and to our children. We cannot demand that our children honor and obey us as they would the Lord if we are not godly people, sensitive to the Lord's direction for our families. Too many parents use Ephesians 6:1-3 as a club to beat the idea of submission into the minds of their children, without ever seeing the bigger picture.

3. But what if the one in authority is not a Christian? In fact, what if he is evil?

Does Ephesians 6:1 create a loophole? "Obey your parents *in the Lord*" (emphasis mine). What if the one in authority is not "in the Lord?"

The phrase "in the Lord" does not modify the word *parents*. Rather, "in the Lord" expresses the realm within which we obey our parents, or anyone else in authority for that matter. A clearer translation of this verse would read, "Children, obey your parents *as you would the Lord.*"

Of course, young people might naturally respond to this by exclaiming, "Hey, wait a minute. My parents are not worthy of that level of respect." They may be absolutely right; however, they need to distinguish between the *person* and the *position*.

Many Americans do not believe that former president Richard Nixon deserves respect because they view him as a lawbreaking liar. That may or not be true of him as a person. Yet, if he walked into my home or yours, we would properly stand and greet him as "Mr. President," not because of his *person*, but because of his *position*.

For years I hated my father. His abuses caused him to forfeit my respect, or so I thought. That would have been true had he been just one of 5.2 billion people in the world. But he was not one of 5.2 billion. He was my father. He was the only person to hold that *position* in my life. As such, he deserved my honor and obedience.

Have you noticed that repeatedly in the Bible God accomplished His plans and purposes through ungodly leadership? He never advocates rebellion as an appropriate response. Our basic ethic can be summarized in the words of our Lord, "Give to Caesar what is Caesar's, and to God what is God's" (Matt. 22:21), even though Caesar's regime eventually executed Him.

4. Doesn't this reduce us to mere puppets on a string, with the one in authority holding the end of the string?

Quite the contrary. Proverbs 21:1 states, "The king's heart is in the hand of the LORD; He directs it like a watercourse wherever he pleases." A proper understanding of the biblical concept of authority does not reduce us to puppets on a string with the one in authority holding the end of the string. In actuality, the one in authority becomes the puppet on the string. And guess who holds the end of the string? That's right! God Himself holds the end of the string.

A careful reading of Scripture reveals a most interesting fact. Often God elevated His choicest servants, not to the number one spot, but rather to the number two position. Nehemiah did not become king, but the cupbearer to the king. Joseph did not become Pharaoh, but second-in-command under Pharaoh. Daniel did not rule over Babylon, but served as an administrator under the King of Babylon. Esther saved an entire nation because she achieved a place of influence next to the king. Has God elevated you to a place of influence in the life of someone in authority over you? Do you have regard for the opinions of your children as people of influence in your life?

5. What should we do when we disagree with the one in authority?

From the preceding discussion, some may conclude that we have only two options—blind obedience or wholesale rebellion. May I suggest a third? In Daniel 1, when confronted with a command that violated a personal conviction, Daniel made a request of the official in charge. In formulating his request he took the following steps.

- He treated the official with proper respect. In Daniel 1:12 he used the word "please" in making his request.

- He determined the reason behind the official's command. "Why should he [the king] see you looking worse than the other young men your age?" (Dan. 1:10) The official's primary concern focused on Daniel's health, not his diet.

- He developed an alternative plan which would answer the concern of the official. "Please test your servants" (Dan. 1:12).

- He made a request which was temporary in scope, rather than asking for a permanent arrangement. "Please test your servants for ten days" (Dan. 1:12). In other words, he offered the official a way out, rather than proposing an agreement which would become etched in stone.

- He made his request and left the results with God (Dan. 1:11-13).

Our children should be taught to respond to our authority in the same way. Three facts must be underscored in their thinking:

(1) Freedom is a privilege, never a right.

(2) Privileges are earned, never demanded.

(3) There is only one way to earn privileges—trust. An attitude of honor coupled with actions of obedience builds trust. We must help them understand that obedience will result in greater freedom, while rebellion will only result in greater restrictions.

6. What if I am adopted or from a broken home? Who then am I obligated to obey?"

I am often asked this question in reference to parental authority. While these situations can at times become rather complex, allow me to venture a simple answer. The young person in question should obey the one who has legal custody of him. My answer comes from an application of Romans 13:1—"Everyone must submit himself to the governing authorities, for there is no authority except that which God has established."

This can get a little sticky, especially when the child spends weekends at a different parent's house. In this case, the rules of the home where he is staying certainly must apply to him while he is visiting, even if he is only there for a weekend.

The Bible also indicates that if a young person is forced for any reason, including death or divorce, to live apart from one or both natural parents, God has a special plan for his life. Moses was raised in Pharaoh's household, apart from his natural mother and father (Heb. 11:24). Joseph was taken from his family while still in his teens (Gen. 37:2). Esther's parents both died when she was a young child (Esther 2:7). Even Jesus fits this profile. Where was Joseph on the day Jesus was crucified? His mother was there. Jesus made provision for her care from the cross (John 19:27). Joseph was nowhere to be found. Most scholars believe that Joseph died when Jesus was much younger.

David has some tremendous words of comfort and encouragement for anyone living in a family situation where one or both natural parents have been removed. In Psalm 68:5, God refers to Himself as "A father to the fatherless." If your children fall into this category, you can rest assured that God has a special plan for their lives.

7. When, if ever, are we justified in rebelling against someone in authority?

As believers, we are never justified in rebelling against those in authority; however, one exception to the principle of obedience does exist. When a person in authority commands us to violate a clear command of Scripture, at that point we must obey God rather than man. In the interests of accuracy, such an action does not constitute *rebellion,* but rather *submission.* The person has chosen to *submit* to the penalty for his disobedience rather than violate his own convictions.

We find a clear example of this in Scripture. The Sanhedrin discovered that Peter and John were preaching salvation through Jesus Christ.

> Then they called them in again and commanded them not to speak or teach at all in the name of Jesus. But Peter and John replied, "Judge for yourselves whether it is right in God's sight to obey you rather than God. For we cannot help speaking about what we have seen and heard" (Acts 4:18-20).

Did Peter have this episode in mind when he penned his words in 1 Peter 2:18-25?

> Slaves, submit yourselves to your masters with all respect, not only to those who are good and considerate, but also to those who are harsh. For it is commendable

if a man bears up under the pain of unjust suffering because he is conscious of God. But how is it to your credit if you receive a beating for doing wrong and endure it? But if you suffer for doing good and you endure it, this is commendable before God. To this you were called, because Christ suffered for you, leaving you an example, that you should follow in His steps.

"He committed no sin, and no deceit was found in His mouth."

When they hurled their insults at Him, He did not retaliate; when He suffered, He made no threats. Instead, He entrusted Himself to Him who judges justly.

If our children are ever asked, by a teacher at school for instance, to violate a clear command of Scripture, they should properly respond by moving through the steps outlined under question 5. If the one in authority does not favorably respond to their requests, then they have no alternative but to restate their convictions and submit to the consequences. We must be ready to support them.

One Last Thought

Over the past few months, several people have shared with me the unbelievably abusive situations they must face every day. Nowhere in Scripture does God demand that we allow ourselves to be used as someone else's punching bag. The principles of honor and obedience do not apply when a person is being destroyed physically or emotionally.

Romans 13:1-7 allows for due process to take place in punishing an evildoer. When a person breaks the law, he must answer to the governing authorities who act as "God's servant, an agent of wrath to bring punishment on the wrongdoer" (Rom. 13:4). If you know of someone living in an abusive situation, either on the job or in the home, please appeal to him or her to contact the proper authorities so that justice can be rendered.

You and I have been handed a golden opportunity to make a difference in our society. By committing ourselves to this seventh conviction, we can maintain a shining example and godly influence in our world. May God help us live in obedience and honor toward those He has placed in authority over us.

God has placed me under authority for my protection and direction; therefore, I must obey those in authority over me, with a joyful attitude, until I am required to disobey the Word of God (1 Sam. 15:23).

Taking Inventory

Are You for Sale?

1. Take a moment to list each of the authorities under which you currently live. As you look over your list, do you respond to each authority with an attitude of honor and obedience? How do you talk about them in your home? Do you possibly communicate to your children an attitude of disrespect by the things that you say, or do you set an example of honor toward those in authority over you?

2. As you talk through these examples with your children, have them make a similar list of their authorities. Have them evaluate their responses to those on their lists just as you have done.

3. Do you consistently obey the law? Remember the seat belt story? Are there times when you communicate to your children a lack of respect for the government? If so, what steps must you take to correct this?

4. The next time you find yourself having to make a request of your authority as Daniel did, use his example. Also use his story as a teaching tool with your own children. Help them to identify times they may have to do the same. At school, for example, they may have to respond to a morally harmful

assignment. How can your experiences help them?

5. Have you ever had to disobey a person in authority because you chose not to violate a biblical conviction? If so, what was the cost? Share this with your family members. In this way you will be motivating them to obey their own convictions even though it may cost them.

Chapter Ten:
MENTAL SUICIDE

*Conviction #8—My brain controls the way I live;
therefore, I must not pollute my mind
(Philippians 4:8).*

"Daddy, I'm scared of the beast." My little Ashley's words
reverberated throughout the theater. I wanted to slide under
my chair.

Everyone thought that she looked so cute squirming
on my lap while grabbing onto my neck. She dug her finger-
nails into my jugular vein as she screamed into my ear over
and over again, "I'm scared of the beast." Her fear-filled face
broke into a big smile as Beauty married the beast—turned
handsome prince.

The kicker came at the end of the movie. As we left
our seats, Ashley pulled on my pant leg and boldly confessed, "I wasn't really scared, Dad. I was just pretending."
Ah ha.

Unfortunately, things didn't end with the movie cred-
its. No sooner had I pulled into our garage than she shrieked,
"I'm scared to get out of the car. The beast might be hiding
in there." For two weeks my wife and I had to walk her to
the bathroom, scout around in her bedroom, and keep the
lights on in the hallway. A couple of times she absolutely
freaked out at the thought that the beast might crawl out
from under her bed and eat her. Many times during that two-
week period I thought of this conviction:

My brain controls the way I live; therefore, I must not pollute my mind (Phil. 4:8).

The Beginning of the End

Unfortunately, fearful fantasies do not restrict themselves to the minds of children. Consider this case in point.

I will never forget the day my hero fell off his pedestal. I now realize that I never should have placed him there in the first place. But at the time I was young, naive, idealistic, and believed the best about everybody. I succumbed to feelings of utter betrayal, shock, denial, and disillusionment as my hero crashed and burned at the base of his pedestal.

My pastor and I first got an inkling of this impending scandal when my hero canceled a series of evangelistic meetings we had scheduled at the church. We then discovered that he could no longer accept any invitations. Before long, the sordid scenarios began to emerge, a trail of deception that caught his family and associates by complete surprise. Another of God's choice servants had been effectively blown to bits within the cozy confines of a motel room.

How did this happen? Any one of us possesses the smarts and the wherewithal to resist a full-blown frontal assault by the enemy, don't we? My hero certainly did. I have a sneaking suspicion, however, that Satan's seductions begin long before we make contact with his beautifully disguised and cleverly baited hook. I have a hunch that our present conviction strikes at the very heart of this most important issue, a hunch that I am determined to pass on to my children:

My brain controls the way I live; therefore, I must not pollute my mind (Phil. 4:8).

The Battle Is On

Does Satan understand the implications that this conviction holds in regard to spiritual attack? You'd better believe it. My hero began teetering on his pedestal long before he took his first steps toward the beckoning bedroom. The moment he left his mind unguarded the satanic seductions began.

No area of compromise is more subtle. And no sellout is more prevalent. I have become shocked at the indifference I sense among so many parents concerning the videos they rent, movies they attend, prime-time television shows they watch, magazines they read, lyrics they listen to, and books they enjoy. I fear that far too many of us have failed to prepare our families for this aspect of spiritual attack.

The four deadly words, "I can handle it," can too easily become our haven and eventually, our destroyer. Consider the following examples.

- Implicit or explicit sexual messages subtly erode our families' convictions, dulling our senses to the fact that those who send these messages are blatantly attacking God's revealed moral will.

- Violence subtly destroys our children's respect for the sanctity of human life. I feel sick when I hear Christian young people talk about the latest movie in which humans get butchered. Have we unwittingly allowed some members of our families to develop an insatiable thirst for blood, guts, and gore?

- Profanity subtly undermines our respect for the character of God. When we become complacent about dragging His holy name in the gutter, we are in serious spiritual decline.

  We cannot handle it!

Our Marvelous Minds

A mere three pounds of pinkish-gray tissue comprise the control center for our movements, sleep, hunger, thirst, and virtually every other vital activity necessary to survival. Composed of approximately 10 billion interconnected nerve cells, our brains control all human emotions, including love, hate, fear, anger, elation, and sadness. The brain also interprets the countless signals it receives from other parts of the body and from the external environment. And this amazing computer of ours fits snugly in that custom-made cavity located between our ears. Lap-tops have nothing on the little MacIntosh you carry around inside your noggin!

The functions performed by these, as Sherlock Holmes would say, "little gray cells" are virtually innumerable. The mind is a marvelous thing—unless it becomes polluted.

As Solomon warned in Proverbs 4:23, "Above all else, guard your heart, for it is the wellspring of life." The "heart" does not refer to the little pump that circulates our blood. Solomon's readers would have instantly equated the heart with their thinking processes (Prov. 23:7, KJV). We must teach our children to guard their minds relentlessly because their every choice springs from their brains.

Jesus expanded this principle in Mark 7:

Again Jesus called the crowd to Him and said, "Listen to Me, everyone, and understand this. Nothing outside a man can make him 'unclean' by going into him. Rather, it is what comes out of a man that makes him 'unclean.' "

After He had left the crowd and entered the house, His disciples asked Him about this parable. "Are you so dull?" He asked. "Don't you see that nothing that enters a man from the outside can make him 'unclean'? For it doesn't go into his heart [mind] but into his stomach, and then out of his body." (In saying this, Jesus declared all foods "clean.")

He went on: "What comes out of a man is what makes him 'unclean.' For from within, out of men's hearts [minds], come evil thoughts, sexual immorality, theft, murder, adultery, greed, malice, deceit, lewdness, envy, slander, arrogance, and folly. All these evils come from inside and make a man 'unclean.' " (Mark 7:14-23).

Unfortunately, the English translation as recorded here does not communicate the emphasis Jesus placed on specific words. A literal, word for word translation of verse 21 reads, "For from within, out of the hearts of men, the evil thoughts come forth, sexual immoralities, thefts, murders. . . . " In other words, Jesus clearly indicated that sexual immoralities, thefts, murders, etc., *result* from evil thoughts. Given enough time, a polluted mind will result in a polluted lifestyle.

The time has come for our families to heed the warning of the Apostle Paul to his young disciple Timothy:

The Spirit clearly says that in later times some will abandon the faith and follow deceiving spirits and things taught by demons. Such teachings come through hypocritical liars, whose consciences have been seared as with a hot iron (1 Tim. 4:1-2).

Satan's spokesmen and women present themselves in a most seductive manner. If we think that his primary medium of communication is somehow related to voices in the night or shadows on a wall, we are sadly mistaken. He loves to elevate people to key places of influence and package his message in their lavish lifestyles and contemptible comments. A television star, professional ball player, or prominent musician generates a far greater following than sinister noises in the night.

Satan really isn't all that smart. We can easily prepare our children to discern his messages. They're readily available in one of three familiar formats. His demonic teaching (1) openly mocks God's name by reducing Jesus Christ to gutter language, (2) openly mocks God's standards by portraying an unrighteous lifestyle that appears abundantly fulfilling with no price tag, or (3) openly praises Satan, by stirring up an attraction to the bizarre.

Such messages have become nightly fare. Glitzy, glamorous stars and starlets blatantly, brazenly, and relentlessly chip away at the Judeo-Christian ethic foundational to our families. America's slab has become cracked and the whole house is in danger of imminent collapse.

One illustration will suffice. During the course of an interview the other night, a rather prominent actress mentioned that in her soon-to-be-released movie she will play a twenty-one-year-old virgin. She then broke out in uncontrollable laughter. When she regained her composure, she looked into the camera and sneered, "A virgin. Can you imagine anyone twenty-one years of age and still a virgin? Why do I get all the weirdo parts?" She broke into laughter again, this time joined by the entire studio audience. Chip, chip, chip.

Once we allow ourselves or our children to become accepting of such messages, we find ourselves dining at the enemy's table, partaking of forbidden fruit.

The Battle for the Mind

The mind absorbs everything it sees and everything it hears. This input can have a direct influence on future choices for years and even decades to come.

By properly programming our children's mental computers, Satan can render them vulnerable to his subtle but certain attack. At the precise moment that their guard comes down, he can punch the playback button, shifting his implanted images into their conscious minds. They win or lose the battle the moment they decide what they will or will not allow to enter their eyes and ears.

Paul set the standard sky high, and rightly so! He wrote, "Finally, brothers, whatever is true, whatever is noble, whatever is right, whatever is pure, whatever is lovely, whatever is admirable—if anything is excellent or praiseworthy—think about such things" (Phil. 4:8). Any subtle sellout concerning this issue could have far-reaching consequences. Just ask my hero.

Blueprint for Victory

Given the fact that we live in a world in which godless messages daily assault our senses can we hope to help our children maintain pure thoughts? Absolutely! But this will require all-consuming commitment and hard work. Consider this five-point plan:

1. We must determine that we will win this battle, regardless of the cost (Heb. 12:4).

The danger in this entire discussion is this—the tendency to minimize the seriousness of a polluted mind. Solomon's words, "Above all else, guard your heart" (Prov. 4:23), appear so placid while lying on a page. We cannot see or hear the intensity with which our Lord would shout these words if He were here to utter them audibly. But let me ask you a question: of all of the commands in your Bible, how many begin with the words, "Above all else?"

This battle requires an all-out commitment, involving every member of the family. We must work together in order to achieve victory.

The classic passage in the Bible relative to spiritual warfare clearly alludes to this subject:

Put on the full armor of God so that you can take your stand against the devil's schemes. . . . Take the helmet of salvation (Eph. 6:11, 17).

Two factors must be noted in order to properly interpret these two verses. First, the phrase "devil's schemes" also appears in Ephesians 4:14: "Then we will no longer be infants, tossed back and forth by the waves, and blown here and there by every wind of teaching and by the cunning and craftiness of men in their *deceitful scheming*" (emphasis mine). Cunning and crafty deceit make up the totality of Satan's arsenal. He understands that by controlling a mind, he can corrupt a life. To let our guards down concerning our minds is to play right into the devil's hand, thereby setting ourselves up for certain destruction.

Second, in warfare the helmet protects the head from a fatal blow. In hand to hand combat one well-placed chop to the head would split the cranium like a watermelon. The helmet would cause the sword to glance off the head, sparing the life of the soldier within.

What then is meant by the phrase, "the helmet of salvation?" Linking the concepts of head protection with salvation, you and I have been biblically mandated to *think the way a saved man or woman ought to think*. We, along with our children, must ask the question, "Do our thought lives reflect the kinds of images about which godly people ought to think as defined in Philippians 4:8?" If not, we leave our minds open to a fatal blow from the enemy.

My hero's eventual demise may well have begun when he simply pushed an inappropriate button on his television's remote control. True, the specifics of his little compromises will never be known to anyone but himself. But the generalities we can surmise for sure. You know as well as I that at some point he dropped his guard.

The writer to the Hebrews gives us a bit of insight into the kind of effort this warfare will demand. "In your struggle against sin, you have not yet resisted to the point of shedding your blood" (Heb. 12:4). Victory demands this level of commitment.

How can we keep our minds pure? We must begin by determining that we will win this battle, no matter what this victory might cost.

2. We must never expose ourselves to mentally harmful messages (Rom. 13:14).

Romans 13:14 states, "Make no provision for the flesh in regard to its lusts" (NASB). *Flesh* refers to our bodies which crave physical stimulation. *Lusts* refers to any physical desire which cannot be righteously satisfied. Thus, the Bible commands us never to place ourselves in a situation that will stir up the lusts of our flesh. *The New International Version* translates this verse with a slightly different, but related emphasis: "Do not think about how to gratify the desires of the sinful nature" [or flesh].

I cannot help but remember Joe, a high school student who experienced agonizing struggles with lust. He came to me with tears streaming down his face as he begged me for help. In our discussion we covered all the usual bases. He did not attend "R-rated" movies. He did not read pornographic material. He tried memorizing Scripture. Nothing seemed to work.

We set up a follow-up appointment for the next week at his house. When I arrived, I took one casual look around his room and could not believe what I saw. Tacked onto his wall, conveniently placed just above his bed, hung a full-color poster of the L.A. Raider's cheerleaders dressed (or undressed) in their skimpy little cheerleader outfits. Bingo! The source of his problem stared him right in the face every night just before he went to bed!

Are you ready for this one? Where do you think he got the poster? His father bought it for him.

3. We must saturate our minds with the Word of God (Rom. 12:2).

One little phrase in Romans 12 provides hope for all of us: "By the renewing of your mind." Over time, the reading and rereading of the Word of God will gradually flush out the accumulated filth that has built up over the years, thereby transforming our lifestyles (Ps. 119:11). Unfortunately, this is not a once and for all proposition. Because our senses are bombarded continually with destructive messages, Bible reading must become a part of our daily lives.

Are you presently involved in any kind of Bible reading program? As mentioned in chapter 4, the goal of reading one chapter per day will enable you to read through the entire New Testament each year. A commitment of just twenty minutes per day can help you begin the process of renewing your mind.

4. We must begin a new mind association (Ps. 1).

Fortunately, our minds can only think one thought at a time. I have yet to meet anyone capable of thinking two completely distinct thoughts simultaneously. Herein lies even more hope for those who struggle with impure thoughts.

As a child, did you ever play a mind association game? You may have begun the game something like this. "Tell me the first thing that pops into your head when I say the word, 'Stop.' " Your partner would then in all likelihood respond by saying "Go."

One of the keys to overcoming impure thoughts is to begin a new mind association. This is how it works. The minute the movie screen in the back of your head gets pulled into place, and the movie projector switches on with some "X-rated" fantasy, respond immediately with a different thought. For me, one of three possibilities will pop into my head:

(1) I think of all of the men in the Bible whose lives ended in destruction and humiliation because they choose to fulfill the fantasy that I feel tempted to enjoy.

(2) I remind myself of the men I know personally who have succumbed to devastating temptations, causing them to reap what they have sown (Gal. 6:7).

(3) I picture Jesus Christ hanging on the cross, paying the penalty for the sins my mind longs to portray.

The minute these associations enter my head, the lure and attraction of my enticing images vanish into thin air. Such is one of the many benefits of biblical meditation (Ps. 1:1-3).

A student asked me just last week, "Can you explain to me what the Bible means by meditation?" The simple fact is that we all meditate. The word simply means to mentally chew on something by running it through our minds over and over again. The problem does not lie in an absence of meditation. The problem involves the object of our meditations. Far too often we find ourselves meditating on the wrong things.

We should aim for the ability to think *biblically*. A new mind association coupled with a regular program of Bible reading should move us a long way toward the achievement of this worthy goal. Begin now to train yourself concerning a new mind association. The very moment you see the screen coming down, allow that recognition to trigger a new, biblical thought.

5. Speak freely with your children about these things (Deut. 6:4-9).

Every semester I counsel more students than I can count regarding their thought lives. Given the sheer numbers involved, I rarely remember individual cases. Steve proved to be one exception. I remember his situation to this day.

Our conversation began normally enough—Steve struggled with lust. I listened attentively, chimed in when I could, prayed with him, shook hands, and walked back to my office thinking to myself, "Dewey, old boy, I'm afraid that you didn't help him very much."

Several weeks later we got together again. When I asked him how he was doing with his battle, his face lit up, and his countenance beamed with excitement. He had made phenomenal progress.

"Well, Steve, you've got to tell me," I said. "What turned it around for you?"

I will never forget his answer. "I went home a couple of weekends ago and had a great heart-to-heart talk with my dad. I couldn't believe it. My dad struggles with lust too! We have decided to hold each other accountable, and together we shall overcome!"

How liberating it is for our children to know that we struggle too. Spiritual battles are commonplace. But our children often feel as if they are the only ones who go through this stuff. I would encourage you to share honestly and openly with the other members of your family about your own battles. We need not get overly specific. Details shared indiscriminately will only hurt our children. Sharing general categories of struggles will prove sufficient. Believe me, our children do not want us to be *perfect*. They want us to be *honest*.

6. When you fail, do not give up (1 John 1:9).

Our society assaults our minds with its sensuous messages virtually every moment of every day. We cannot ingest this amount of material, innuendo or otherwise, without experiencing some measurable effect. We must not, therefore, give up at the first sign of failure.

God designed the dynamic of confession for just these sorts of battles. When we face our failure as honestly as God does, we will experience His cleansing "from all unrighteousness" (1 John 1:9).

Our sins grieve the Holy Spirit (Eph. 4:30). Biblical confession should call our sins into account with the same level of grief that God experiences. When that happens, the sheer sorrow that we feel should motivate us more strongly to resist the temptation the next time around. Thus, when we fail in the area of our thought lives, or any other area for that matter, we should always confess but never give up.

If only my hero had listened to himself preach. I know that he knew this material. I have heard him expound on this stuff over and over again. But talk is cheap. His little compromises eventually destroyed him.

Solomon understood. "Catch for us the foxes, the little foxes that ruin the vineyards, our vineyards that are in bloom" (Song of Songs 2:15). As the little foxes ruin the vineyards, so our little compromises can ruin our lives. Just ask my hero.

My brain controls the way I live; therefore, I must not pollute my mind (Phil. 4:8).

Taking Inventory

Are You for Sale?

1. Solomon commanded us to "Above all else, guard your heart, for it is the wellspring of life" (Prov. 4:23). How well do you guard your heart? What magazines, books, videos, music, etc., do your children observe you watching or reading? Must any changes be made?

2. Until reading this chapter, how serious have you been about keeping your mind pure? What steps have you taken in the past to guard your family from morally harmful information? What new steps will you include in your battle plan now?

3. Do you regularly saturate your mind with the Word of God? Since reading chapter 4 of this book, have you noted any measurable improvement? If you have begun to fall back on commitments that you made, now would be a good time to renew your commitment to reading your Bible.

4. In what ways does your family make provision for the flesh? Is this an area of concern? List any areas of compromise that come to your mind and then decide what steps you must now take.

5. Do you regularly watch any television shows that you now see as harmful? If so, take your television guide and, together with the members of your family, cross off those programs. How about movies? Are there any that you were planning to see, but now will not? Do you have any magazine subscriptions you must cancel, or videos you must toss? This house-cleaning must begin with you.

6. Why not discuss with your children what you have done? Talk over with them the utter importance of all of this. Help

them to evaluate their own viewing and listening habits.

7. Encourage your children to take the same steps that you have with their own magazines, tapes, etc. Remember, this will be far more meaningful if you have first set the example and if your children feel some ownership in this decision. Do not just force your will on them. Allow them time to digest all of the material in this chapter and to arrive at their own conclusions and responses. Acting as their prompter rather than their master will prove far more beneficial in the long run.

Chapter Eleven:
WALKING ON OUR KNEES

Conviction #9—Without Jesus Christ I can do nothing;
therefore, I must live my life in daily dependence
upon Him (John 15:5).

When little Tommy walked into his Sunday School class, he looked so sad. Miss Taylor, one of the most sensitive teachers in our church, took one look at him and asked, "Tommy, is anything wrong?" It didn't take much to open the floodgates. He began to sob uncontrollably.

Tommy's mother and father had separated the year before. The divorce hit Tommy like a sledgehammer because he loved his daddy so much.

Tommy hadn't seen his dad for three months when finally the phone rang and it was him! "Hey Tommy, how about you and me going camping next week?" his father asked. "I'll pick you up on Saturday morning around ten, and we'll drive up into the mountains and spend the night in a tent. We can go hiking, and I'll bring a kite for us to fly. What do you think?"

Tommy couldn't believe it. He was so excited that he told all his friends at school. He got a big black felt-tipped pen and began to cross off the days on his calendar one by one as he waited for Saturday to arrive.

Finally the big day came. Tommy was packed and ready to go. He counted the minutes until ten o'clock as he waited in front of the big window.

At first Tommy figured that he just got delayed loading the car or something. At eleven o'clock he thought that maybe his dad had really said, "I'll pick you up at eleven," and that he heard "ten" by mistake. By noon, Tommy didn't know what to think. So he prayed, "Dear God, please bring my daddy here quickly." But his father never came.

Miss Taylor never expected the avalanche of emotion and confusion that she received when she asked Tommy if anything was wrong. Tommy carried an enormous load of pain into his Sunday School classroom. He felt totally abandoned and betrayed, not only by his father. Tommy also felt totally abandoned and betrayed by God.

"Why didn't God answer my prayers, Miss Taylor? You told me that God loves me and wants the best for me. My mom prays with me every night before I go to bed. She told me once that God loves to answer the prayers of little boys. Why didn't God bring my dad to my house yesterday? I don't think my dad loves me anymore. Doesn't God love me anymore either?"

If you were Tommy's mother or father, how would you have answered his questions? What would you have said to Miss Taylor if she had asked you, "Why would God allow a little boy as sweet as Tommy to hurt so badly like that? Why didn't God just answer his prayers?"

Prayer has fallen on some hard times. I believe that I can pinpoint the reason.

Admittedly, there are many subjects, the mere mention of which would cause people to sit up a little straighter and focus their eyes a little keener. Anticipation seems to be built into a whole spectrum of subjects. Prayer is just not one of them.

I have seen this in the eyes of my college students. "Today, we're going to talk about dating." The room breaks into a chorus of buzzes and whispers. Notebooks fly open. My students sit with pens poised and paper at the ready as they hang on every word. Yet, when I begin class by saying, "Today, we are going to talk about prayer," most students slouch against the backs of their chairs. A few hearty yawns punctuate my points. Why? I have a theory.

A Dying Dynamic

I am operating from a clearly defined premise—"We Christians do not pray much." Yes, some notable exceptions exist. But for the most part, prayer seems to have become the dying dynamic of the Christian life. I have certainly noted this tendency among my Christian college students, most of whom, by the way, come from fine Christian families.

Most books on the subject attribute prayerlessness to a lack of discipline. Since prayer requires concentration and effort, it only makes sense that we have to work at effective praying. Anything which requires hard work can easily become neglected. Or so the reasoning goes. I do not agree, however, that lack of discipline is the culprit.

Prayerlessness among Christians seems especially curious given the overtures the Bible ascribes to prayer. "The prayer of a righteous man is powerful and effective," wrote James (James 5:16). Do we not want our lives to be powerful and effective? Then why do we not pray more?

"Do not be anxious about anything, but in everything, by prayer and petition, with thanksgiving, present your requests to God. And the peace of God which transcends all understanding, will guard your hearts and your minds in Christ Jesus" (Phil. 4:6-7). In a day in which stress seems to rule the roost, we would think that Paul's words would strike a familiar and much-longed-for chord in each of our hearts.

Jesus' words sound especially tantalizing. "And I will do whatever you ask in My name, so that the Son may bring glory to the Father. You may ask Me for anything in My name, and I will do it" (John 14:13-14). There you have it—a blank check. Note the two key words, *whatever* and *anything*. Those terms just about cover it all, don't they? As long as we pray "in Jesus' name," the sky's the limit. Or so it seems.

Yet the sad fact remains—many of us, and many of our children, do not pray. Why?

Ready or not, here's the answer. Many of us have tried prayer only to conclude that it simply does not work. We would never admit this publicly. Such an assertion sounds almost blasphemous. Nevertheless, I have talked to students by the dozen who have asked me in all sincerity, "Since God is going to do whatever He's going to do, why do I need to pray?" Sometimes they phrase the question a bit less theologically and a bit more realistically: "Why do I need to pray when so many times I do and nothing seems to change?" You know as well as I do that if every time we prayed for something, and "Poof," we got the answer, we'd pray by the hour, regardless of the discipline required.

Many well-intentioned teachers have attempted to skirt the issue by trying to get God off the hook. "Well," they point out, "God does always answer our prayers. It's just that He answers with 'yes, no, or wait.' " Others only succeed in placing us on the hook when they say, "If you had more faith, the answer would come. The problem here is not with God but with you." That certainly brings comfort to an anguished soul! Try laying that one on Tommy.

Evidently, such teachers overlook the fact that James said, "When you ask, you do not receive" (James 4:3). Thank God that James included that verse! At least we have here the biblical possibility that we can pray and not receive.

But what do you say to someone whose aunt lies dying in a hospital bed? This person kneels beside her ailing aunt and cries out to God in sincere faith, "Dear God, you know I love my aunt. Please God, heal my aunt. Give the doctors wisdom in diagnosing her problem. May her body respond to the medication. And in Jesus' name, please restore her health."

Two hours later the phone rings. "We are so sorry to inform you that your aunt has died." What sensations flood this person's heart? Betrayal, abandonment, resentment? Where are the "whatevers" and the "anythings" now?

As human beings, we are notorious for needing immediate, positive reinforcement. Having tried prayer in the most traumatic of circumstances have we given up because prayer seemingly does not, as the bumper sticker states, "change things"? For our children's sake, as well as our own, we need to face this dilemma head on.

Dependent, but on Whom?

Prayerlessness in the lives of believers becomes especially grievous when we understand that our humble, daily dependence upon God is best measured by the barometer of our prayer lives. As our conviction states:

Without Jesus Christ I can do nothing; therefore, I must live my life in daily dependence upon Him" (John 15:5).

If we have become virtually prayerless, then our actions may well betray a dismal reality. Perhaps we have shifted the object of our dependence away from God, only to become dependent on ourselves.

The Disciples' Dilemma

If you feel convicted by all of this, please don't be too hard on yourself. Apparently the disciples struggled with some of this as well. Note their request in Luke 11:1—"One day Jesus was praying in a certain place. When he finished, one of his disciples said to him, 'Lord, teach us to pray.' " Surely they noticed a quality in Jesus' prayer life that was uncharacteristic of their own.

Jesus responded to the disciples' request by rehearsing for them what we commonly call "The Lord's Prayer." While an abbreviated version appears in Luke 11, Matthew records for us the extended rendition in Matthew 6. For any of us who have ever wondered why prayer does not work, "The Lord's Prayer" emphasizes one extremely important fact. The problem does not lie with the *concept* of prayer, but rather with the *content* of our prayers.

A Literary Masterpiece

Volumes have been written on the subject of prayer. No treatment of the topic comes close to the comprehensive scope and practical nature of Jesus' fifty-two-word statement. His sample prayer covers every conceivable subject about which an individual might want to pray, including delinquent daddys and ailing aunts.

You will note that the prayer is circular, rather than linear. Rather than starting at point A and taking us to point B, the prayer ends exactly where it begins. The prayer builds to a crescendo, each statement riding piggyback on the preceding one. A literary masterpiece indeed!

Six specific requests comprise this prayer. In this chapter we will consider the first three in detail, leaving the last three for your own family study and discussion (although I will give you enough clues to get you started).

What an opportunity God has given us! Can you think of anything more worthwhile than teaching our own children how to pray?

Praying Jesus' Way

Jesus did not intend for us merely to memorize the prayer and quote it from rote. Such a practice would violate His words in Matthew 6:7, "Do not use meaningless repetition" (NASB). Rather, Jesus gave us a pattern by which we must organize our prayers. Each request constitutes a category. By following this outline, we can teach our children how to experience "powerful and effective" prayer lives.

Before we consider the six requests, please note the introduction of the prayer—"Our Father in heaven" (Matt. 6:9). Do you sense a balance here? By approaching God as our father, we can enjoy intimacy with Him. My little Ashley loves to climb up in my lap and talk me through her entire day. We can enjoy the exact same kind of intimacy with our God anytime we want. Yet, He is our Heavenly Father. We must maintain a distance. My children call me "Daddy," never "Dewey" or, as my students say, "The Dew Meister." We must never treat God in a flippant, familiar, casual way. "Intimacy balanced with respect" describes our proper approach to God.

We come now to the categories themselves. As these unfold, you will see how our prayer lives do indeed reflect our sense of utter dependence on God, for without Christ, we can do nothing.

Category #1: The Motivation of Prayer

Do you remember James 4:3? James said, "You do not receive, because you ask with wrong motives." Jesus zeros in on that possibility right out of the shoot when He begins His prayer, "Hallowed be Your name" (Matt. 6:9).

You have probably quoted those words from memory on occasion. But do you know what they mean? As an imperative in the original language, this verse should read, "Make Your name hallowed," or "holy." Thus, our prayers should begin with the thought, *Father, make Your name holy.* Such describes the *motivation* of prayer.

You will not be surprised to learn that we live in a world that does anything but regard our God as holy. Our society mocks His standards, violates His truth, blatantly flaunts its wholesale rebellion in His face, and blasphemes His name by reducing "Jesus Christ" to gutter language. Surviving in such a hostile environment stretches our children's emotional and spiritual reserves to the limit.

Thus, when we close the door and find ourselves alone with God, the all-consuming, passionate desire of our hearts ought to express itself with the words, "Father, make Your name holy, both in my world and in my life." In displaying His holiness we live in daily dependence on Jesus Christ, for without Him we can do nothing.

When I served as a youth pastor, I desperately wanted to build this passion into the hearts of my young people. I can remember regularly walking around the perimeter of the schools in my neighborhood as I cried out to God, "Lord, give me this campus." By that I meant, "Jesus, allow Your voice through my influence to become the dominant influence on this campus this year." I now long to build this passion into my children and teach them this conviction.

Our desire to see God elevated as holy ought to color everything else for which we pray. When our children sense this passion burning in our own hearts, they will begin to understand why effective, powerful praying begins with this attitude.

Frankly, many of the prayers to which I have been exposed over the years seem to be motivated more by a passion for creature comforts than God's holiness. If my observation is indeed accurate, no wonder our churches limp along in impotent fashion, and our children perceive prayer incorrectly. I fear that our collective Christian focus has become distressingly skewed.

Category #2: The Evangelization of Prayer

When Isaiah saw God lifted up as holy, he fell at His feet and proclaimed, "Woe to me. I am ruined" (Isa. 6:5). Such should be the response when people see Him lifted up as holy today. This leads us to the second dimension of "The Lord's Prayer," the *evangelization* of prayer — "Your kingdom come" (Matt. 6:10).

Most commentators believe that this request is eschatological in nature. In other words, we are to pray for the Second Coming of Christ and the establishment of His future millennial kingdom. Such a view overlooks two pertinent facts, however: (1) Jesus would never encourage us to pray for His Second Coming when the first coming was still in progress; (2) There would be no reason to pray for His kingdom to come at the very moment He was offering His kingdom to Israel. This request has nothing to do with the future, but has everything to do with the present.

What do you need to have a kingdom? You need two things — a king, and subjects to the king. Question: What happens when someone recognizes that Jesus Christ is the King of Kings and Lord of Lords, and willingly submits his life to Him? Answer: He becomes a Christian.

Do you see the progression in this prayer? After asking God to elevate Himself as holy in our lives and in our world, we then should focus on all of our friends and loved ones who do not know Christ as King of kings and Lord of lords. We should beseech God to manifest His kingdom in their hearts.

As a family, can you name the unsaved people God has placed in your lives? Do you pray for them regularly? Are you passionately consumed with a desire to see them rightly respond to the King of kings and Lord of lords? Have you become actively involved in their evangelization by asking God daily to set Himself apart as holy in your lives?

This aspect of prayer, if faithfully observed, will build into the hearts of our children an intense burden for the lost. May it be true that in their own hearts they cry out on behalf of their unsaved friends, "Your kingdom come." In this we live in daily dependence upon Jesus Christ, for without Him we can do nothing.

Category #3: The Submission through Prayer

We now come to the heart and soul of this prayer. "Your will be done on earth as it is in heaven" (Matt. 6:10). This request should immediately trigger a question in our minds — "How is God's will done in heaven?" His will is done immediately and completely. We ought to desire to do His will in the same way.

As we consider the *submission* through prayer, the time has come to define the word *prayer*. Much confusion and pain would be spared the "little Tommy's" of our world if we defined prayer with accurate terminology. "Prayer is NOT you and me asking God for what we want. Prayer IS discerning what God wants, and that is what we ask for." God never intended prayer to reduce His Son to a sanctified Santa Claus. Yet, far too many of us respond to Him in exactly this manner. Do our children relate to Him in this way as well?

Let me put it another way. The bumper sticker reads, "Prayer changes things." Bad theology. The primary purpose of prayer is NOT to change things. The primary purpose of prayer IS to change you and me. The bumper sticker was correct so far as it went. But it left out the center of the equation. Prayer changes us. And as we change, things change.

One final definition should suffice. "Prayer is that dynamic of the Christian life whereby we take our stubborn, selfish, self-centered wills and bring them into submission to God's will." This answers the question, "If God is going to do whatever He's going to do, then why do I need to pray about it?" We do not pray about a situation in order to change the situation. We pray about a situation in order to change our hearts' response to the situation. And as our hearts change, often, but not always, the situation will change.

"What about Moses?" someone will ask. "Didn't God change His mind in response to Moses' prayer?" On the surface of things, the answer would appear to be, "Yes." The Scripture reads, "Then the LORD relented and did not bring on His people the disaster He had threatened" (Ex. 32:14).

Did God "change His mind" as the *New American Standard Bible* records? Such phraseology falls under the heading, "Anthropomorphism," in which God's actions are described in human terms. God does not "change His mind." Such an action would violate His immutability. In Numbers 23:19, Moses (who also wrote Exodus 32:14, by the way), states, "God is not a man, that He should lie, nor a son of man, that He should change His mind."

What exactly happened, then, in Exodus 32? The answer is simple. When God saw the stubborn, rebellious heart of Israel, His attribute of justice blazed against His wayward nation. But when Moses, leader of Israel, revealed a broken and contrite heart, God's attribute of mercy kicked into gear. God's character did not change. He merely responded to a changed heart with the appropriate attribute.

We are left with one last thorny problem. What about Jesus' promise in John 14:13-14? The entire discussion hinges on the phrase, "in My name." We have tacked those words on the end of our prayers as some sort of divine "Abracadabra," or as my daughter would say, "Ah la peanut butter sandwiches," as if ending our prayers "in Jesus' name" makes them more effective. Yet, you will not find one prayer in the entire Bible that ends "in Jesus' name."

Jesus spoke those words, recorded in John, to His disciples on the night before His betrayal. To a Jewish mind, a person's name held a far greater significance than it does to an American mind. We typically choose a name based on its sound. As we read through a baby name book, certain names catch our fancies, while others don't sound quite as cute. How "Dewey" fits into this discussion I'm not quite sure, but you get the idea. A Jew would never choose a name based on its sound, but rather on its meaning. In fact, names were occasionally changed to coincide with the change in a person's character or circumstances, such as the time God changed Abram, "exalted father," to Abraham, "father of many" (Gen. 17:5).

To the Jews, a person's name represented the totality of that person's character and attributes. His name expressed the sum total of all that he was in a one word designation. Thus, Jesus' words had an entirely different meaning to the disciples than they do to us. They would never have applied His statement by merely ending a prayer "in Jesus' name."

Let me rephrase Jesus' words as the disciples would have understood Him. "And I will do whatever you ask *when you pray the way I would pray if I were here,* so that the Son may bring glory to the Father. You may ask Me for anything,

praying the way I would pray if I was here, and I will do it."
How appropriate, considering the fact that within the next
twenty-four hours Jesus would be gone.

Prayer does indeed change things, but only because
prayer first and foremost changes us. And as we change, things
change. In submission to His will we live in daily dependence
on Jesus Christ, for without Him we can do nothing.

Practicing the Proper Pattern for Prayer

Your aunt falls prey to a terminal disease. Distressed, you
turn to the only resource you have at a traumatic time such
as this. "Dear Father, You know how much I love my aunt. I
cannot bear to face life without her. She practically raised me.
I owe my life to her. Please reach down and touch her body,
and restore her health. In Jesus' name, Amen." You pray
sincerely, in faith, believing, and you pray in Jesus' name. But
the phone rings. You are greeted with the news, "Your aunt
has died." How do you feel? Betrayed, abandoned, ignored, as
if God dangled a carrot in front of you, only to snatch it away
when you dared to reach out to Him?

Or, your aunt falls prey to a terminal disease. Distressed, you cry out to God: "Dear Father, You know how
much I love my aunt. I cannot bear to face life without her.
She practically raised me. I owe my life to her. Many people
will be coming by her hospital bed today—doctors, nurses,
loved ones, and friends. I pray that even in the midst of her
tragic circumstances, through her godly responses, others
will see you as holy. And as these people see You as holy,
may the testimony of my aunt draw many of them into Your
kingdom. And Father, You know how desperately I long to
have her healed. If You choose to heal her, I will rejoice in
that. But if, within the perspective of Your plans and purposes, You choose to take her home, I will rejoice in that as
well. Not my will, but Yours be done."

Sound familiar, like something Someone prayed one
night in a garden? The phone rings, "Your aunt has died."

Now how do you respond? Grieved, sorrowful, broken-hearted, but rejoicing.

Do you see the difference in the two prayers? The one only breeds resentment as God fails to deliver on a self-centered request. The other results in sorrow for the loss, should the aunt die, but acceptance in the belief that God's will has been done. Trusting God to fulfill His plans and purposes, even when things go differently than we desire, constitutes praying in faith, believing indeed!

Concluding Prayer Categories

You are now ready to tackle the remaining three categories. As promised, I will aid you with a couple of clues.

Category #4: The Provision of Prayer

"Give us today our daily bread" (Matt. 6:11). Typically, most of our requests fall into this category. Prayers for jobs, cars, physical ailments, family stresses, etc. would be included here. We can properly pray for these things, but only after filtering them through the grid of the first three categories.

As you consider discussing this category with your children, answer these leading questions.

(1) Why do you suppose Jesus listed a request for our provisions as #4, rather than #1? Think through the progression of the prayer. Do we not run the risk of praying for our needs, motivated by greed rather than His holiness?

(2) How can we properly pray for items such as a car, keeping in mind the first three categories of prayer?

(3) What is the significance of the phrase, "daily bread?" Why didn't Jesus say, "monthly meat?"

Category #5: The Confession of Prayer

"Forgive us our debts, as we also have forgiven our debtors" (Matt. 6:12). As you prepare to teach this aspect of prayer to your children, several questions must be considered.

(1) Why does this category appear as #5 on the list? Does His provision of our needs in some way reveal our own unworthiness to receive His blessings, given our sinfulness in comparison to His holiness?

(2) Since He has already forgiven all our sins, past, present, and future (Rom. 5:1; 8:1), why do we need to ask for forgiveness now? Or does the Bible speak of two different kinds of forgiveness? See 1 John 1:8-10 for further information.

(3) If we do not forgive those who have hurt us, does this request mean that God will not forgive us? How can this be? What does the one have to do with the other? Consult Matthew 18:21-35 for this one.

Category #6: The Protection of Prayer

No single category has more significance for our children than this one. This aspect of prayer alerts them, and us, to potential spiritual attack as we ask God for His protection. "And lead us not into temptation, but deliver us from the evil one" (Matt. 6:13).

We have now come full circle, for as we fend off Satan's seductions into sin, we maintain our integrity, thereby setting God apart as holy in our lives. We are right back where we started. What a marvelous prayer!

Prayer does indeed serve as the most accurate barometer of our dependence upon Jesus Christ. Yes, prayer has fallen on some hard times. So has our dependence on God. May the discussion of this conviction rekindle our passion to see His holiness manifested in the midst of a world that frankly couldn't care less.

Without Jesus Christ I can do nothing; therefore, I must live my life in daily dependence upon Him (John 15:5).

Taking Inventory

Are You for Sale?

1. Describe your own prayer life in twenty-five words or less. What can you conclude about your sense of dependence on God in light of your prayer life?

2. Have the members of your family do the same. Has prayer been a vital part of their lives, or a neglected aspect? Discuss the matter together.

3. Think back over the last week. About what items have you faithfully prayed? Make a list of every request that you can remember. Now compare this list with the outline in Matthew 6. Have you been praying correctly? Does the content of your prayers match the categories as outlined in "The Lord's Prayer"? Have the members of your family do the same exercise.

4. Have you fallen into the trap of subtly concluding that prayer simply does not work? Or have you seen evidence of "powerful and effective" prayers in your life? Does this chapter change or reinforce your thinking in any way? If so, how?

5. Each aspect of this prayer is worthy of the investment of one week. Why not start with category #1, and as a family creatively look for ways to live out this request in your lives? You might ask family members to keep a journal, recording specific incidents in which God's holiness was displayed in their lives. Next week, move to #2. In this way, a nebulous prayer can be transformed into vivid and specific reality.

6. Especially emphasize the information under category #3, "The Submission through Prayer." Share together as a family the ways in which your prayers are changing you. Enable the members of your family to note specifically any changes in their lives. Nothing will energize one's prayer life more than realizing that prayer does indeed change us!

7. Do you remember little Tommy waiting for his father? If

he were your son, how would you seize this experience as a "teachable moment"? How would you instruct him to pray? What lessons would you teach him from this? How could you, as his parent, assure him that Jesus has not abandoned him, but rather loves him very deeply and shares the pain that he feels, having Himself felt rejection many, many times? (John 1:12) How would you pray for your son in this situation? Use the example of little Tommy to seal in the minds of your children the proper application of the principles discussed in this chapter.

Chapter Twelve:
SUFFERING FOR JESUS' SAKE

*Conviction #10—Jesus Christ loves me so much that
He hung in my place and took the blows that were meant
for me; therefore, my greatest privilege is to stand
in His place and take the blows that are meant for Him
(Colossians 1:24).*

Modern-day martyrs are hard to find, at least in this country.
I consider myself uniquely privileged to know one. His name
hardly qualifies as a household word. He has yet to make the
cover of *Christianity Today* or *Moody Monthly*. But he
wouldn't want that anyway.

Kevin became a rather prominent presence on the
junior high and high school campuses in his city. A pied piper
of young people, his exact location could always be pinpoint-
ed. He usually stood in the epicenter of a quaking gathering
of students. He spoke with them as friend to friend in his
attempt to motivate them toward holy living.

Kevin became directly responsible for countless
young people turning away from drugs and turning to Jesus
Christ as the solution to life's problems and pressures. He
held up the Bible as the guidebook they should follow in
making lifestyle choices. He taught his students respect for
authority and counseled kids to make a positive difference on
their campuses and in their communities.

No wonder Kevin was misunderstood. Some of the
school administrators couldn't answer the question, "What's
in it for him?" Some parents shrieked at the thought that
their sons and daughters might fall under the spell of this

"religious fanatic." When the ACLU hinted at the possibility of investigating this apparent breakdown of the "separation of church and state," that was too much.

Once the local newspapers got wind of the story, the chicken was thrown into the fan, the feathers flying everywhere. Reporters showed up in force at the next school board meeting.

"We're not trying to destroy a wholesome and meaningful influence on our campuses," one school board member was quoted, as he proceeded to destroy a wholesome and meaningful influence on his campuses. "Let it be known that this board opposes sin," another added, as if that had anything to do with the issue at hand. "This board of education is not and will not single out Kevin for any wrongdoing," another chimed in, just before making a motion that Kevin be banned from the schools. The editors had a heyday with this one.

The parents, en masse, supported Kevin, while a small but equally vocal minority demanded the removal of anything or anyone that smacked of religious influence. You can guess the result. Kevin got canned.

That's not the half of it. Some people felt so threatened by this one youth pastor's moral voice that Kevin's family was subjected to harassment in the form of crank phone calls, two death threats, menacing letters, and a barrage of blatantly false accusations. Quite a price to pay for just trying to help kids.

What kept Kevin from cashing in his chips and pursuing another avenue of gainful employment? Just ask him, as I did not long ago.

"Some people think I'm stupid, and I've wondered that myself at times. But one verse has kept me going throughout this whole ordeal. Paul's words in Colossians 1:24 have become my hideaway: 'Now I rejoice in what was suffered for you, and I fill up in my flesh what is still lacking in regard to Christ's afflictions, for the sake of His body, which is the church.' I guess when you picture in your mind what

Christ suffered for me, what I've gone through for Him is nothing. Absolutely nothing."

Kevin, you are one of whom it can be said, "The world was not worthy of them" (Heb. 11:38).

Confusion at the Cross

"Hey, what's the big deal?" a student challenged me. "Tons of guys got crucified. So He had some thorns pressed into His head. So what? And the nails in His hands? Hey, it only lasted six hours. Some guys get tortured for days, or weeks even. Why do you make such a big deal about this Jesus guy anyway?" I sat dumbfounded at the brashness and arrogance of this high school student's statements.

But all emotions aside, does this young person's comment have any validity? Can the Crucifixion be reduced to a mere six hours of thorns and nails? Or was there something more?

What exactly did Jesus suffer on the cross? Certainly crucifixion was not uncommon in Jesus' day. Men by the thousands experienced the torturous agonies to which Jesus was also subjected. But Jesus' crucifixion entailed much more.

Why do we, and our children for that matter, need to take a second look at the Crucifixion? Because, in the words of both Kevin and the Apostle Paul, our willingness to suffer for Jesus flows directly out of an understanding of Jesus' suffering for us. I firmly believe that the degree to which our children comprehend the significance of the cross, will influence their ability to stand firm in the face of compromise.

In preparation for our journey of discovery, let me first make you a promise and give you a brief warning.

The promise: I will not rehearse for you the details of crucifixion. Much ink has already been spilled concerning this gruesome subject. I need not become redundant. And besides, the physical beatings and torture of our Lord are not the focus of this chapter. We will go beneath the surface to the real issue at hand.

The warning: We shall arrive at our conclusions in a roundabout sort of way. While you may feel at times that we have digressed far off course, please be assured that the whole discussion will come together near the end of this chapter, as we consider together the conviction of the chapter.

Jesus Christ loves me so much that He hung in my place and took the blows that were meant for me; therefore, my greatest privilege is to stand in His place and take the blows that are meant for Him (Col. 1:24).

Setting the Stage

Have you ever desired to write a best-selling book? If so, I have a piece of advice for you. Do not write a book about hell.

Most people do not like to read about the eternal torment of human beings. I can't blame them; neither do I. In fact, if God had given me permission to write the Bible, I would have omitted a number of verses.

Would you like to read a few? Check out Matthew 25:41, 46:

Then He will say to those on His left, "Depart from Me, you who are cursed, into the eternal fire prepared for the devil and his angels."

Then they will go away to eternal punishment. Or how about Revelation 20:10, 14-15?

And the devil, who deceived them, was thrown into the lake of burning sulfur, where the beast and the false prophet had been thrown. They will be tormented day and night for ever and ever.

Then death and Hades were thrown into the lake of fire. The lake of fire is the second death. If anyone's name was not found written in the Book of Life, he was thrown into the lake of fire.

To be completely honest with you, I have mentally mud-wrestled over the biblical concept of hell. Certain questions have assaulted my thinking. "How can a loving God send someone to hell? Why does the torment of hell have to be eternal? Why doesn't God simply annihilate a person?"

These and other equally troublesome questions will no doubt rattle around in the minds of your children some day, if they haven't already. An up-close and personal discussion concerning these issues might prove invaluable to your family, not to mention the fact that it will indeed lay the foundation for a proper understanding of our present conviction. If you do not yet see the connection, keep reading.

The Raw Realities

The Bible presents five clear and indisputable facts concerning hell, each equally indispensable to our understanding of our present conviction.

1. Hell is a place prepared by God for the devil and his angels (Matt. 25:41).

When God originally conceived of a place called "hell," He did not intend for people to go there. He prepared hell for "the devil and his angels." Why?

Ezekiel 28:12-19 gives us our first eyewitness account of Lucifer (whose name means "light" or "shining one") before his defection into the ranks of God's archenemy. A perusal of these verses reveals that this "anointed cherub" possessed radiant beauty and blameless perfection.

Isaiah 14:12-14 reveals the shocking nature of Lucifer's rebellion. Five times he utters the two deadly words, "I will," climaxed by the declaration, "I will make myself like the Most High" (v. 14).

Satan attempted to seduce as many angelic beings as possible into following his diabolical schemes. Revelation 12:4 indicates that ⅓ of the myriads of angels joined hands with

Lucifer. We now know them as demons. He next moved into the arena of the human race and has since terrorized the world as "the god of this age" (2 Cor. 4:4).

I have no problem accepting the fact that this diabolically evil creature will find himself consigned to the Lake of Fire forever.

2. Hell is a place reserved for every human being who lives his life in rebellion against God (Rom. 2:4-6).

Even though God did not originally prepare hell for people, Romans 2:4-6 contains a most ominous warning:

> Or do you show contempt for the riches of His kindness, tolerance and patience, not realizing that God's kindness leads you toward repentance?
> But because of your stubbornness and your unrepentant heart, you are storing up wrath against yourself for the day of God's wrath, when His righteous judgment will be revealed. God "will give to each person according to what he has done."

With these words, the apostle drew a line in the sand. He successfully divided the human race into two distinct categories: the obedient and the rebellious.

Please note the definitions of two key words. *Stubbornness* refers to the attitude of someone who might say, "I know that what I am doing is wrong. But I'm going to do it anyway." *Unrepentant* carries this thought one step farther. "I know that what I am doing is wrong. But I'm going to do it again and again and again."

Keep in mind that these people have set themselves against the plans and purposes of God. They have declared their own moral independence and have chosen to live by their own ethical standards regardless of the revealed will of God.

Every rebellious act committed by such an individual

represents a deposit in the Bank of God's Wrath. At the appointed time, the account will be closed. Then payday will come. "A man who remains stiff-necked after many rebukes will suddenly be destroyed—without remedy" (Prov. 29:1).

Does this sound too harsh? Then consider this thought. If Satan, who as an angel possesses at least some measure of the supernatural, deserves an eternity in Hell due to his highhanded, willful, defiant rebellion, then how much more must a mere mortal deserve the same destiny and doom?

3. Hell is an utterly terrifying place (Luke 16:23-28; Matt. 13:47-50).

The story of the rich man and Lazarus provides us with a tremendous insight into the goings on in the horrifying halls of Hades. Admittedly, some would seek to relegate this story to the level of a parable, thereby suggesting that we should not interpret this passage literally. Such an argument overlooks two facts, however. First, a parable never uses proper names; this story certainly does. Second, a parable presents a spiritual truth in a story-like fashion. The principle must be interpreted literally even if the events within the story are not.

The rich man retained his consciousness. He did not experience soul sleep. Nor was he simply annihilated. He maintained his faculties and remained abundantly aware of his circumstances.

Apparently, and I stress the word *apparently*, the rich man was alone. Certainly others were there. But no mention is made of any dialogue or contact took place between the rich man and the others. I mention this point of aloneness only because several young people have told me over the years, "I would rather be in hell with my friends than in heaven without them. With my friends there, we'll have one ongoing, never-ending party!" How naive. Not only did the rich man find no parties, but he apparently found no friends.

He experienced an agonizing existence. Listen to his

anguish as expressed in Luke 16:23-24:

> In hell, where he was in torment, he looked up and saw
> Abraham far away, with Lazarus by his side. So he called
> to him, "Father Abraham, have pity on me and send
> Lazarus to dip the tip of his finger in water and cool my
> tongue, because I am in agony in this fire."

A great gulf separates those in hell from those in
heaven. The Bible clearly states, "Between us and you a
great chasm has been fixed, so that those who want to go
from here to you cannot, nor can anyone cross over from
there to us" (Luke 16:26).

Missed opportunities and foolish choices may contribute significantly to the anguish of hell. "But Abraham replied,
'Son, remember that in your lifetime you received your good
things' " (Luke 16:25).

Jesus' "Parable of the Net" in Matthew 13:47-50 adds
a bit more color and definition to the horrors of hell. Jesus
spoke of the certainty of the coming judgment (v. 49), the
comprehensive nature of the judgment (v. 49), and the character of the judgment (v. 50).

Jesus warned, "There will be weeping and gnashing
of teeth" (Matt. 13:50). The weeping reveals a relentless
anger. Have you ever experienced such anger that you broke
into convulsive sobs? The gnashing of teeth expresses an
unbridled fury against God. Surely you have known those
who, in a fit of rage, tighten their jaws and grind their teeth.

Hell will be anything but a party. The venom of a
person's hatred toward God will spill off his lips throughout
the endless ages of eternity.

4. Hell is deserved (Rom. 1:20).

Here's a point for your family to ponder: How many people
will God send to hell?

Answer: Absolutely none.

For whatever reason, on this particular issue, God gets a lot of bad press. People frequently ask, "If God is so loving, how can He send good people to hell?" Why does such confusion exist concerning such a basic reality? The Bible addresses this issue in the clearest of terms. God sends no one to hell. Every person who winds up in hell does so for one unmistakable reason — he chooses to be there.

The Bible reveals, in several passages, just how hard a person's heart can become toward God. For this discussion, we will examine three passages. Consider allowing these examples to stimulate some meaningful discussion with your children concerning their own hearts' attitude toward God.

Revelation 9:18-21. As you read these verses for yourself, please keep two facts in mind. First, these events will occur in the future. If you know Jesus Christ, you will be long gone before they ever happen. Second, God, like a loving father spanking a disobedient child, is using every means possible to persuade men and women to turn back to Himself. He would far rather subject them to temporary pain now that an eternity of torment tomorrow.

If only they would say, "OK, God, You win. I turn from my rebellion." God would immediately turn off His wrath like you turn off a faucet. But note their response. After unprecedented plagues strike the earth, "the rest of mankind . . . did not repent" (v. 20).

Like an irritating skip in a phonograph record, the words "did not repent" occur again and again throughout these passages, expressing a defiant, unrepentant rebellion.

Revelation 16:1-11. As you read through this unbelievable list of indescribable disasters, do you think these events would arrest the attention of these people? Guess again. "They were seared by the intense heat and they cursed the name of God, who had control over these plagues, but they refused to repent and glorify Him" (v. 9). In verse 11 we read that they again, "cursed the God of heaven" and once again "refused to repent of what they had done."

Revelation 6:12-17. If only these people would direct a prayer of repentance heavenward, the plagues would come to a screeching halt. Read this passage in Revelation 6 carefully. The people pray all right, but notice to what they pray—"the mountains"! (v. 16) And listen to their prayer: "Fall on us and hide us from the face of Him who sits on the throne" (v. 16). "Anything but Jesus Christ!" That's their cry.

How should God respond to such a prayer? Should He tie a rope around their necks and drag them kicking and screaming into the kingdom? I think not. Indeed, every person who winds up in hell does so by his or her own willful, defiant, hard-hearted choice.

You might ask, "But can't a person choose to repent once he finds himself in hell?" It isn't that he *can't* repent once he's in hell. He *won't* repent once he's in hell. The torments of hell continue throughout eternity because a person's rebellion against God continues throughout eternity.

How does God respond to all of this? Does he act like a boy who pulls the wings off a moth and he enjoys watching the creature wiggle in pain? Hardly, though admittedly some people have just such a conception of God. Read Jeremiah 9:1 and 14:17. Like rivers of water flowing from His eyes, God will weep tears of sorrow throughout eternity.

Just imagine. God loves you and me so much that He will allow us to rebel if we choose to, rather than drag us against our wills into the kingdom, even though our choices will consign Him to an eternity of weeping.

5. One last fact remains concerning hell. Hell is deserved by me, and by you.

For the first seventeen years of my life I lived in wholesale defiance against God. I hardened my heart, clenched my fist, and refused to bow my knee to Him or to anyone.

But God refused to abandon me. He did one last thing. He said, "I will become like him and die in his place. Will that get his attention?"

In all my years of speaking at youth camps and conferences, I have never focused the attention of a crowd on the gory details of the Crucifixion. Yes, the tortures Jesus experienced there were excruciating. Christ suffered the full fury of the wrath of men so that men would never have to suffer the full fury of the wrath of God. I would never minimize that. Yet, crucifixion was hardly uncommon. Men by the thousands were subjected to such horrors.

But please note this. The agony of Jesus' suffering did not result primarily from a soldier's whip, but from His Father's wrath. Listen to Jesus' anguished cry as He screamed, "My God, My God, why have You forsaken Me?" (Mark 15:34) In that awful moment, God the Father literally rained down on His Son the white-hot lava of His wrath, scorching Him in your place and mine. In a way that I cannot explain to you Jesus literally became "sin for us, so that in Him we might become the righteousness of God" (2 Cor. 5:21).

While on the cross, Jesus addressed His Father as "My God." Every other time He prayed, He addressed Him as His Father. But while on the cross, Jesus did not relate to God in intimacy as a son to His father, but rather as an object of His wrath. In that sense, our sins ripped the Trinity.

In one unspeakable moment, all of the hellish torment that I have described in this chapter, multiplied by 5.2 billion people, multiplied by an eternity of time came crashing down on Jesus in concentrated form. A brash and arrogant high school student's question notwithstanding, I doubt if He even felt the crown of thorns at that point.

Jesus faced the eternal fire prepared for the devil and his angels.

Jesus suffered the "stored up wrath" awaiting every stubborn and unrepentant person who clenches his fist and shakes it in God's face.

Jesus felt the agonizing torment described by the rich man who longed for someone, anyone, "to dip the tip of his finger in water and cool my tongue, because I am in agony in this fire" (Luke 16:24).

Jesus took on Himself the punishment that we so rightfully deserve while He stood innocent.

Jesus paid my penalty in my place, even though for seventeen years of my life I hated His guts.

And Jesus did it all for one very simple yet profound reason—He loves us. Indeed, it is almost as if God loves you and me more than He loves His own Son, because He did not spare His own Son so that He could spare you and me.

Jesus Christ loves me so much that He hung in my place and took the blows that were meant for me; therefore, my greatest privilege is to stand in His place and take the blows that are meant for Him (Col. 1:24).

In the midst of that broad road that leads to destruction (Matt. 7:13-14), God has erected a huge cross. The "many" who walk that road must face that cross and make a determined choice to walk around it before cascading into the Lake of Fire.

Did that cross get my attention? You'd better believe it. I took my hardened heart and softened it. I took my clenched fist and opened it. I took my rigid knee and bent it. I have never been the same.

A New Perspective

Christ's suffering did not end on the cross. People hated Him then; they hate Him today. He remains the object of the wrath of men, even as we speak.

Our children certainly understand this. Just listen to some of their friends talk. The name "Jesus Christ" continues to season the speech of most everyone, from a grammar school student playing on the blacktop to the most vile and profane pervert walking the streets of Hometown, USA.

Something has changed, however. Jesus Christ is no longer here to receive the brunt of the blows. That's where you and I come in.

Paul revealed a most interesting perspective concerning the subject of persecution, one with which Kevin identified perfectly:

Now I rejoice in what was suffered for you, and I fill up in my flesh what is still lacking in regard to Christ's afflictions, for the sake of His body, which is the church (Col. 1:24).

Need I remind you that Paul wrote those words while wallowing in a dungeon?

For the moment, focus on the word *rejoice*. Biblical rejoicing has nothing to do with some fickle emotion of happiness. It has everything to do with a deep down confidence that no matter what we may be going through, no matter how difficult it may be, God remains in control. You and I can rejoice in the midst of the most painful persecution because we are literally filling up in our flesh "what is still lacking in regard to Christ's afflictions" (Col. 1:24).

Do we understand the significance of these words? Do our children? Kevin certainly did. Every time you and I suffer because of our commitments to Jesus Christ, we move one step closer to bringing Christ's afflictions to completion. What a privilege!

Jesus Christ loves me so much that He hung in my place and took the blows that were meant for me; therefore, my greatest privilege is to stand in His place and take the blows that are meant for Him (Col. 1:24).

Taking Inventory

Are You for Sale?

1. Our conviction begins with the words, "Jesus Christ loves me so much that He hung in my place." Using the topic of hell as the foundation, discuss with your children just how

much Jesus Christ truly does love us.

2. The three passages in Revelation graphically illustrate the degree to which someone can harden his heart. Use these examples to warn your children of the consequences of a hardened heart. Keep in mind that you do not want to scare them. Adapt the details of the biblical descriptions to the ages of your children. The focus should not be placed on the plagues or catastrophes, but rather on the unwillingness of the people to repent and give God glory.

3. Kevin clearly understood that he will never suffer anything that compares to the suffering of Christ on the cross. Discuss this aspect with your children. Does this not give us a new motivation and boldness to stand for our convictions no matter what the cost?

4. Can you list any opportunities that you may have had to suffer persecution because of your faith in Christ? Use these examples to encourage your children to take their stand even when it becomes painful to do so.

5. If you cannot think of any examples under #4, then ask yourself, "Why not?" Have you compromised when the pressure was on? Do you not have any relationships with ungodly people? Is your lifestyle indistinct? These and other soul-searching questions may provide you and your family with a golden opportunity to discuss this whole matter of suffering for Jesus' sake.

6. Help your children to anticipate the times they may have to stand against the flow and discuss the price they may have to pay in the process. Compared to the price Jesus paid, is He asking too much when He calls on us to be faithful?

Part Three
Making Our Choices

Do the words "So what?" haunt you as they do me? We began this book by contrasting *hypocrisy* with *integrity*. We further developed our discussion by considering ten biblical convictions. So far, so good. But "So what?" How does this material help us make everyday decisions? In a word, how can we apply what we have learned to the so-called "gray areas," those myriads of situations for which we have no verse of Scripture? In this final section, we shall attempt to answer this question.

Chapter Thirteen:
DEWEY'S DREADFUL DILEMMA

Would you believe it? I finally found a command in the Bible that I have no trouble obeying. This thing's not even a temptation. I've got this one completely under control. Any ideas? Check out 1 Corinthians 8:10: "For if anyone with a weak conscience sees you who have this knowledge eating in an idol's temple, won't he be emboldened to eat what has been sacrificed to idols?"

Now be honest. Do you struggle with eating meat offered to idols? I sincerely doubt it. On the surface, the entire eighth chapter of 1 Corinthians may seem completely culturally irrelevant. Yet "all Scripture is God-breathed" (2 Tim. 3:16), so why did the Holy Spirit include this chapter in the Bible?

In order to fully understand the intent of Paul's admonition to the Corinthian believers, I must first point out two extremely important facts:

(1) The Bible clearly declares certain issues as absolutely right or absolutely wrong. For example, should we lie, steal, pay our taxes, love our wives, commit adultery, or faithfully attend a Bible-believing church? Without a moment's hesitation, you would answer "no, no, unfortunately yes, yes, no, and yes." Wouldn't life seem simple if we could

find chapter and verse for every decision of life?

(2) Unfortunately, the Bible does not address many of the issues we face daily. What would you say to someone who asked you, "Should I or should I not attend movies, dance, smoke, wear makeup, play the lottery, own a VCR, or listen to 'Rock' or 'New Age' music?" No matter how strongly we may feel about any of these issues, we can search the Bible from cover to cover and we will simply find no verse.

How do we make rational choices concerning these so-called "gray areas"? Typically, many people have approached such issues from one of two possible perspectives. Neither is completely correct, and both can be equally damaging.

Two Options

Legalism. Legalists believe that while God had ten commandments, He unfortunately neglected a few; therefore they must help Him out. This view presents a problem—which commandments do we include on the list? Some would add "Thou shalt not dance," while others would feel that dancing is acceptable, but gambling of any kind (including the lottery) must be avoided. More important, when pressed to defend their positions, legalists have no biblical basis for their views. They have no verse and therefore no credibility. Oh sure, they may twist some verse out of context to support their views. But many, if not most, young people can instantly recognize these manipulations. Consequently, young people often reject the legalists' standards outright.

Libertarianism. Those who hold this view would endorse any behavior not expressly forbidden in the Bible. They would teach that because the Bible nowhere says, "Thou shalt not smoke," we have the liberty in Christ to "flick our Bics." I suppose that since my *Strong's Exhaustive Concordance* nowhere lists *Rock Cocaine,* we can go for that as well.

So how do I make choices? The answer does not lie within the bounds of legalism or libertarianism. Rather, the solution centers around one key biblical term: *discernment* (Phil. 1:9, NASB, translated "depth of insight" in the NIV).

Neither legalism nor libertarianism teach our young people anything. Legalism places them in straight jackets with no biblical basis, while libertarianism only leads to anarchy and ultimate self-destruction. Discernment allows our sons and daughters to think critically while filtering every decision through a carefully constructed biblical grid.

Now for the $64,000 question: "How can I teach my children discernment?" At this point, allow me to beat a fast retreat back to 1 Corinthians 8.

Idol Burgers, Anyone?

"Gray areas" are nothing new. They have been with the church since its inception 2,000 years ago. Only back then they did not deal with such things as movies or makeup. Believers in the early church split over the issue of eating meat offered to idols. Some felt that an idol was nothing more than sticks and stones, so they didn't mind buying the sacrificed, choice meat at cut rate prices.

Others were not so quick to jump on the idol burger bandwagon. They wanted nothing to do with any aspect of idol worship. Some superstitiously believed that they would become demon possessed by eating the meat. (Don't laugh. A Christian radio talk show host announced to a horrified audience that he had uncovered a diabolical plot. Apparently, the high priests of the Church of Satan had placed a curse on trick-or-treat candy, giving some high ranking demons permission to possess any child who ate the satanized Sugar Babies. We had people threatening to picket our annual Harvest Party in protest.)

The Guidelines

Paul dealt with the disturbance in masterful fashion. Far from being culturally irrelevant, 1 Corinthians 8 illustrates one un-

mistakable fact: the Bible provides us with the guiding principles we need to make discerning decisions concerning virtually every questionable activity we may encounter. In this
chapter, we shall consider seven such guidelines.

1. Is this activity beneficial, or potentially damaging to my body or my mind? (1 Cor. 6:12)

Early on in their careers, athletes learn the raw realities of
life — "No one will ever remember how we begin. They will
only remember how we end." Last week I watched two
teams scurry all over a grass-covered diamond, locked
together in a grueling pennant race. With ten games to play
and a mere ½ game separating these ball clubs, tempers
flared and passions sizzled. Why? Because two weeks from
now, no one will care about the guys who lose their division.

I don't know about you, but I do not want to end my
life a loser. Neither did Paul. Hence his words:

> Do you not know that in a race all the runners run, but
> only one gets the prize? Run in such a way as to get the
> prize. Everyone who competes in the games goes into
> strict training. They do it to get a crown that will not
> last; but we do it to get a crown that will last
> forever. . . . I beat my body and make it my slave so that
> after I have preached to others, I myself will not be
> disqualified for the prize.

The two phrases *strict training* and *beat my body*
ought to leap off the page at us. The Bible nowhere portrays
the Christian life as a tiptoe through the tulips. We will find
ourselves embroiled in hand-to-hand combat against unseen,
demonic forces with the eternal destinies of billions hanging
in the balance. Victorious Christian living demands a commitment to strict discipline relative to lifestyle choices, lest we
end this contest disqualified.

Consequently, when facing a situation not specifically

mentioned in the Bible, we must ask ourselves, "Is this activity beneficial, or potentially damaging to my body or my mind?" Paul wrote, "Everything is permissible for me—but not everything is beneficial" (1 Cor. 6:12). The word *permissible* refers to any issue not expressly forbidden in Scripture. In other words, *permissible* encompasses any activity for which the Bible has no verse. Such activities may be permissible, but are they beneficial?

While we should never stand in front of a group of young people and declare, "Thou shalt not go to movies," because there is no verse to that effect, we should readily declare that there are countless movies we must never attend. We do not have the luxury of reading just any magazine or book. Most videos we simply dare not rent. We cannot run the risk of polluting our minds.

We should not go some places. An honest, up-front evaluation would reveal the potential of permanent damage, a risk we cannot allow ourselves to take.

This entire discussion comes down to one basic thought: if an athlete, competing for a mere marble trophy, willingly exercises strict discipline, how much more should we do so because we are fighting in the one battle that really counts? Couch potato Christianity accompanied by a loosey-goosey morality must no longer characterize the blood-bought church of Jesus Christ.

2. Would this activity cause anyone to question my commitment to Jesus Christ? (Rom. 2:24)

Paul's rebuke of his Roman readers demonstrates the devastating consequences and far-flung repercussions of believers who violate their integrity. "God's name is blasphemed among the Gentiles (a term often used to refer to unbelievers) *because of you*" (Rom. 2:24, emphasis mine).

What do a bank, some beer, and a Unocal gas station have in common? Let's see if you can discern the common denominator.

While cashing a paycheck at my local branch of the Bank of America, the teller inadvertently gave me $10 too much. Or so I thought. I counted the money, noted the mistake, and promptly whispered up a prayer, "Thanks, God, I can sure use the extra dough." As I turned to walk away, I felt a twinge of conscience. Fortunately, I have learned to follow my instincts, rather than argue with them. I went back to the counter, laid a ten dollar bill in front of the teller, and said, "I'm sorry, but I believe that there's been a mistake. You gave me ten dollars too much."

She smiled and replied, "I know."

"You know? What do you mean, 'I know'?"

"I know who you are," she said with a smirk. "I visited your church last Sunday night. I listened to you speak about honesty. I just wanted to see if you really practiced what you preached." Judas sold Him out for thirty pieces of silver. I just about betrayed Him for $10.

My dad and I were just about to bite into the best looking pizza you have ever seen when he suddenly informed me, "Wait. I just can't eat this pizza without a can of beer." He promptly threw me $20 and asked if I would get him a six-pack.

Several thoughts raced through my mind. *My dad must give an account to God, not me, for the choices he makes. I want to be a servant to my dad. He is legitimately sick and cannot get the beer himself. It's his money, not mine. Perhaps I can find a store two cities away where no one will see me with the beer.*

I found a store and bought the beer. As the box boy handed me the bag, I looked up to thank him, and found myself staring into the eyes of a student from my youth group. He didn't say, "Hi, Dewey, how are you doing?" like he usually did. No chance. He shot me a glance that would have melted steel as he fired this verbal arrow right through my heart: "I know that you have a logical explanation for this."

He caught me. Fortunately, he had the confidence in me to say what he did. Do you suppose that someone could have seen me who did not assume that I had a "logical explanation for this"? Might he determine that because the youth pastor apparently drinks, it must be OK for him? By allowing myself to be seen in a somewhat compromising situation, might I have caused another to sell out?

My son and I were motoring our way up Highway 14 to our home when I noticed that I needed to stop for gas. Since the Unocal station sat right off the freeway, we pulled in. My car was thirsty all right, $14.50 worth of thirsty. When I went to pay the bill, the attendant handed me a receipt for $7.50. I thought to myself, "Hey, hey, hey, today's my lucky day." As I signed the receipt, I felt that nagging twinge of conscience. "I'm sorry," I reluctantly replied, "but there's been a mistake. I pumped $14.50 into the car."

She swore at the computer and apologized. "Ah, we've been havin' problems with the pumps lately. What would you like me to do?"

"If it's not too much trouble, could you write me out a new receipt?"

"You are joking, aren't you?" she asked, the dismay evident in her voice.

"I know it's a pain," I sympathized, "but could you write out a new receipt?"

As she handed me the corrected version, she looked both ways to make sure her boss could not hear her. She then leaned over the counter and asked, "Why did you do that? No one would have known."

"Ma'am," I answered, "I would have known." As we got back into the car, it suddenly dawned on me that my son had been standing at my side, taking this all in. At ten years of age, I know what he was thinking. *Dad, for seven bucks we could get some ice cream!* But what will he be thinking when he remembers this little episode someday as a fifteen-year-old? If I had cashed in on a gasoline attendant's honest mistake, I would have programmed an ethical standard into my son's computer software package: "David, stealing is only wrong if you get caught."

Can you see the common denominator in these stories? Each placed me in a situation where wrong responses could easily have caused people to question my commitment to Jesus Christ. Have you faced any similar scenarios lately?

3. Could this activity place me in a situation where I might be tempted in an area of personal weakness? (2 Tim. 2:22)

When he exhorted his young disciple Timothy to "Flee the evil desires of youth, and pursue righteousness" (2 Tim. 2:22), Paul chose a broad term that refers to "any desire which cannot be righteously satisfied." We all have areas of weakness. The discerning believer will readily identify his and avoid tempting situations like the proverbial plague.

I personally have no conviction concerning co-ed swimming ("mixed bathing" as it is called in some parts of the country). However, I have had some very sincere students in my office begging me for help. These guys struggle with an almost overwhelming load of lust. One young man, who was saved out of an extremely immoral background, broke down and wept as he admitted to me, "Every time I look at a girl on this campus, I begin to mentally undress her. I want so badly to treat these girls with respect. What do I need to do?"

Can you anticipate a part of my answer? "John, don't you dare go anywhere near that pool."

Bars have never been an issue with me. While growing up in an alcoholic's home, I grew to detest even the smell of liquor. "Happy hour" places no spell on me whatsoever. (I do, however, have other areas of weakness, I can assure you.) I recently read the tragic story of a former alcoholic who came to Christ while on the pro-golf circuit. He gave up drinking cold turkey. One day he walked into a Sunday morning church service where the Lord's Supper was being served. He did not realize that the communion cup contained real wine rather than grape juice. One sip was enough to send him spinning right back to the bottle. Ten years of victory suddenly blew apart at the seams.

What are your areas of personal weakness? Do you ever place yourself in situations where you might be tempted in these areas?

4. Would Jesus feel comfortable participating in this activity if He were here? (1 John 2:6)

Please resist the temptation to relegate this question to the realm of the trite. In every sense of the word, Jesus is very much right here. No, I am not referring to His omnipresence; yes, I am referring to His indwelling. Because we have already dealt with this concept in detail (please review chapter 6), one brief illustration will suffice in framing this guideline for our consideration.

As a youth pastor, I sat through countless camp talks dealing with teenager sexuality. I cannot begin to estimate how many times I have heard the speaker say something like this: "And when you are tempted to get into the backseat of your car with your boyfriend or girlfriend, you'd better remember that Jesus is sitting on the dashboard, looking into the backseat, watching everything you are doing." Such imagery never did much for me or for the young people in my youth group. At worst, such warnings sounded pretty hokey. At best, the speaker only motivated my students to hang a curtain in the car between the front and backseats. Bad theology never motivates someone toward good morality.

Question: Is Jesus sitting on the dashboard, looking into the backseat?

Answer: No.

Question: Well, where is He then?

Answer: Because Jesus lives in our hearts, He climbs

in the backseat with us. By virtue of His indwelling, He goes wherever we go and does whatever we do (remember 1 Cor. 6:15-20?); therefore, we must ask ourselves, "Would Jesus feel comfortable participating in this activity if He were here?"

5. Would I want my son or daughter to get involved in this activity? (Ex. 20:5)

Much ink has been spilled concerning Exodus 20:5. On the surface, the principle contained in this verse does not seem fair: "You shall not bow down to them or worship them; for I, the LORD your God, am a jealous God, *punishing the children for the sin of the fathers to the third and fourth generation of those who hate Me*" (emphasis mine).

Why would God judge children for the sins of their parents? Such a question, though certainly a natural response to this verse, misses the primary intent of this passage. I do not believe that God zaps grandchildren and great-grandchildren because of what their ancestors may or may not have done. Rather, this verse demonstrates the power of the principle of influence. The lifestyle choices you and I make will have a direct or indirect influence on the choices our children make, even to the third and fourth generations.

One day I took my children to my grandmother's house. As I looked around the living room, the meaning of Moses' words in Exodus 20:5 suddenly leapt into focus. Present in that room that day were my grandmother, my mother, me, and my two children, a grand total of four generations. Do you get the point? My grandmother's lifestyle has a direct *influence* on my children, even though they are generations removed. Consequently, as I consider my choices concerning questionable activities, I must ask myself if I want my children to become involved in these things.

Not only do children tend to do what their parents do, but they usually manage to go one step beyond us. Two illustrations come to mind. The first involves a heartbroken father who discovered to his horror that his son was smoking marijuana. When he came into my office, his eyes flared as he tried to lay the blame on my poor leadership within the youth group. As he verbally berated me for thirty minutes, he chain-smoked seven cigarettes. When the barrage ended, I asked him as tactfully as I knew how, "With all due respect, what is the difference between what your son is doing and what you are doing? He just chose a different leaf."

A leader in my church threatened to have me fired when he learned of his sixteen-year-old son's immoral life-style. In the course of trying to determine what went wrong, I asked him and his wife if he had any pornographic material in the home. He shouted at me, "Of course not. I'm insulted that you would even insinuate such a thing." His wife subsequently jabbed her husband in the ribs with her elbow. Being the trained professional that I am, I immediately recognized her response as a clue.

"I cannot help you or your boy if you are not completely honest with me," I pointed out.

"Tell him about the videos, Harry," was his wife's reply.

Clearing his throat, and looking somewhat crestfallen, he admitted, "Well, I do bring R-rated videos home for us to watch as a family. But I always fast forward past the bad parts." I must acknowledge that my response was most inappropriate and disrespectful. I began to clap and herald him as a pillar of righteousness in our church and in our community.

The principle of influence can be one of the most powerful parenting dynamics. Everything we say and everything we do in some way can contribute to the ethical value system we build into our children. Before you engage in any activity for which the Bible has no verse, please ask yourself, "Do I want my son or daughter to become involved in this?"

6. Could this activity become addictive? (1 Cor. 6:12)

The Bible says nothing about playing the lottery. "Oh," the legalist will say. "You are gambling if you play." "Bad stew-

ardship of God's money," another will cry. Playing the lottery
in my state will cost the participant $2. I have met those who
will quickly decry the evils of the lottery, but they rush to
mail their "Reader's Digest Sweepstakes" before the dead-
line. "Well, playing the Sweepstakes doesn't cost anything,"
they explain. Wrong. Playing the Sweepstakes will cost the
price of a postage stamp. So is the issue the amount of money
at risk?

I do not play the lottery for a far different reason:
addiction. I grew up under a Keno table in Vegas. Every
weekend, off we went. I love the sights and sounds. Something comes over me that I cannot describe. Every fiber within my soul screams out for a chance to beat the odds. Gambling for me has become addictive. I cannot handle it. Consequently, I don't buy lottery tickets.

I do not smoke. The Bible does not say that I will go
to hell if I smoke. I may smell like I did, but there is no
verse. I do not smoke because I watched in amazement one
day as my father literally tore the house apart as he looked
for a cigarette. Couch cushions went flying, silverware scattered across the floor, mattresses were flung in every conceivable direction. Finally, he found a crinkled up, smashed,
two-inch-long tube of tobacco. How he lit the thing I will
never understand. Both hands shook uncontrollably. Finally,
he managed to light one end while madly sucking on the
other, and . . . "Ah," a calmness crept into his face as he
heaved a sigh and collapsed in his chair in front of a Forty-
niner game. I was not a Christian. I didn't know the Bible
from *Moby Dick* or Moses from the Man in the Moon. I only
knew that I would rather die than become a slave to a two-
inch-long leaf.

7. Could my involvement in this activity cause another believer to violate his own convictions? (1 Cor. 8:13)

We have now come full circle. Remember the meat-offered-
to-idols controversy with which we began our discussion

in this chapter? Paul readily acknowledges that (1) "an idol is nothing" (1 Cor. 8:4); (2) "food does not bring us near to God" (v. 8); (3) "we are no worse if we do not eat, and no better if we do" (v. 8); but (4) we cannot allow our freedom to eat the meat to "become a stumbling block to the weak" (v. 9).

Unfortunately, we Christians do a fair amount of "weaker brother bashing." Some of us bemoan the fact that we have matured to a point where we recognize our liberty in Christ, yet we cannot do some things simply because of Mr. Weak Brother over here who is crimping our style because he has not yet arrived at our level of spiritual maturity. Wrong perspective. Do you realize that we are all the "weaker brother?" We simply have different areas of weakness. Understanding this fact, Paul appeals to a greater principle: the principle of *deference,* limiting my freedom so that I do not cause another to violate his convictions.

> When you sin against your brothers in this way and wound their weak conscience, you sin against Christ. Therefore, if what I eat causes my brother to fall into sin, I will never eat meat again, so that I will not cause him to fall (1 Cor. 8:12-13).

As a youth pastor, I never sponsored a dance. Over the years I have seen too many young people receive Christ from immoral backgrounds. Several have confessed to me that in their minds, dancing and immorality are inseparably linked. Every Friday night of their teenaged lives they went to the disco to find their partners for the evening. Like ringing a bell in front of Pavlov's dog, sexual temptation became for them a conditioned response to the sights and sounds of the dance hall. Can you even begin to imagine the devastation and confusion I could create if I turned the fellowship hall into a Friday night dance extravaganza, complete with strobe lights, spinning disco balls, and a Christian rock band? I, for one, will not take the risk.

Summary

The Bible is a masterpiece of literary genius. No other book in all the world can boast the comprehensive scope of the Word of God. Thank God for placing in our hands the blueprint for abundant, victorious living. Even concerning subjects about which the Bible seems silent, principles abound that enable you and me to make discerning choices. May the seven principles discussed in this chapter contribute to the continued fulfillment of Paul's prayer for the Philippian believers:

> And this is my prayer: that your love may abound more and more in knowledge and depth of insight, so that you may be able to discern what is best and may be pure and blameless until the day of Christ, filled with the fruit of righteousness that comes through Jesus Christ—to the glory and praise of God (1:9-11).

Taking Inventory

Are You for Sale?

1. Before we can begin to teach these seven principles to our children, we must first make certain that we are trying to live by them. As you read through the chapter, did any of the seven leap out at you as an area needing improvement? What steps will you now take to ensure that each of these seven principles characterize your own pursuit of discernment?

2. I have attempted to illustrate each guideline with examples from my own life. These will be of limited value and interest to your children. Can you develop your own list of illustrations for each principle? Your children would much rather learn these insights from your life.

3. You and your spouse should talk through a variety of ways that you can reinforce these guidelines to your children. Perhaps you can take one per week for the next seven weeks

and concentrate on making each principle come alive in your own family.

4. Be sure to regularly share with one another both your successes and failures in trying to apply these guidelines to your lives. Be patient. In some cases, you may find that you are developing a whole new grid through which future choices will be filtered. There is no substitute for time when trying to build a new mind-set.

5. Can you name the "gray area" decisions your children are facing every day? This chapter may provide you with a golden opportunity to get inside your children's world and begin to fully understand the pressures they are under.

Epilogue

Both of my children have the chicken pox. I have never had them.

Jesus defined love as one laying "down his life for his friends" (John 15:13). Does a dad "taking five shots of gamma globulin in his derriere because of his kids" qualify?

For whatever reason, David and Ashley seem much more philosophical during an illness. Perhaps they just direct a greater amount of their kinetic energy to their brains instead of their feet since they don't feel like running around much. We have already had some great conversations.

My little Ashley perched herself on my lap. (Just try having your kids do that to you after you have been speared five times by a nurse who said she threw javelins during college. Ah, the story of my life!) She kind of got this faraway look in her eyes, and asked, "Dad, remember when we went to Sea World? How did they get Shampoo (you know, the whale) to do all those funny tricks? What did they feed him after he jumped in the air? Chocolate ice cream?"

Another sick day David and I watched in rapt attention as the crew of the starship Enterprise thwarted a Klingon attempt to conquer the planet Vulcan. As the theme song faded into the background, David looked at me and said,

"It would sure be fun to be a starship captain someday. Dad, what do you want me to do when I grow up?"

I have learned that many of our children's questions are merely expressions of childhood curiosity without much significance. A few questions, however, require a careful, thoughtful response. This was one of those. I realized that my answer might shape the rest of his life.

I thought for a moment and said, "David, I really don't care what you *do* in terms of your career. I only care about what you *are* in terms of your character. I want you to grow up to be a man who knows what you believe, why you believe it, and refuses to compromise what you believe no matter what the cost."

"Do you know anyone like that, Dad?"

"A few," I answered.

"Well, can you tell me about some?" he inquired.

This story came to my mind. Written by a Ugandan pastor, his tale of woe vividly illustrates the point of this entire book. He tells about a rather prominent family who visited his church during a Sunday morning worship service. Like any good pastor, he, along with one of his elders, decided to drop by during the week to thank them for coming. What happened next forever changed his life, and mine. May his words challenge you as they have so challenged me.

The Okelos lived in a large white stucco mansion on Nakasero Hill and we arrived at their home in the late afternoon as the sun was just setting over the valley. A blossoming flame tree stood at their front gate and a wall of hibicus shrubs enclosed the well-kept flower gardens of their enormous yard. The entire atmosphere was one of aristocratic affluence. As we walked to the front door I began to wonder if I was dressed properly and I tried to think how I would begin my message.

The door was half open. We knocked and stepped inside. Beneath our feet was a beautiful light green carpet. A zebra skin hung in the hallway and through the door of the sitting room I could see colorful batiks and expensive European furniture.

We waited for our host for several minutes. No one came to welcome us. When we called out a greeting, there was only silence. I began to think we had come to the wrong house and I turned to my friend to suggest that we leave. Just at that moment a small boy appeared in the doorway of the sitting room. He stood completely still and his arms were raised straight in the air.

Even in the half-light of the hallway I recognized the child as Okelo's youngest son. I moved towards him, strangely moved by his haunting appearance and deeply puzzled. He began to cry and tried to speak but his words were lost in sobs. Before I could reach him he fell completely stiff to the floor.

I bent down to pick up the child. As I did, I looked beyond him into the sitting room. A deep shock passed through my body. The curtains were open and the sun was shining through onto a carpet covered with blood and excrement. Broken teeth and eyes pulled from their sockets were scattered throughout the room. On a table in the center of the floor three human tongues were laid out in a row, as if on public display.

Without thinking I grabbed young Okelo from the floor and with the elder I ran shaking and trembling from the house. The short distance to our parking space seemed to be many miles and with every sound I thought myself a dead man. Finally we reached the car, and I laid the boy on the back seat. The elder and I took our own seats in deep fear and I drove quickly towards my home. Throughout the trip the boy remained motionless, his arms raised rigidly over his head.

When we arrived at the house I put Okelo on a couch and stared helplessly at his paralyzed body. His hands were cold and his eyes stared straight ahead, seeing nothing. Later I learned that he was the sole survivor from a nightmare of death. Soldiers from the army of Idi

Amin had come to his home late in the evening. They had raped his mother and tortured to death each member of his family. Twelve-year-old Okelo was somehow overlooked. When the killing was over and the soldiers had left, he crawled under his bed. He had stayed there for more than a day, his mind empty and his body paralyzed. It wasn't until he heard our voices in the hallway that he had been able to move.

Now, once again, the boy's body was stiff, his mind completely closed to human contact. I tried to comfort him but no words or gestures could reach him. There was no sign of life in his eyes. In utter frustration I picked up my Bible and began to read out loud. I read chapter after chapter. I read of the Christ who promised to see His children beyond the grave. I read of the Redeemer who claimed that the words of His mouth were life and spirit. My own words failed me. I could make no interpretations. I had nothing to say to the small shattered life lying before me. I did not think that the truths I meditated on every morning could reach his deaf ears.

When I looked up from my reading, Okelo was lowering his arms. His neck was no longer stiff and he turned his head to look at my face. There were tears in his eyes but beyond his tears there was life and hope. He looked away again, breathed deeply and closed his eyes.

I took Okelo's hand in mind and prayed to God, thanking Him for His providential care. I confessed my own astonishment. I knew it was in spite of my unbelief that the child responded; it was in spite of my skepticism that God's Spirit had come among us. Now I wanted to cry out, like Peter, "Depart from me; for I am a sinful man, O Lord" (Luke 5:8).

The healing of Okelo was complete. Later that night I drove him to the Kijomanyi Children's Home and he was admitted to the home as a ward of the foundation. When I saw him again the following day he was playing soccer in the yard, running and shouting with the other children. He made many friends and before long he adjusted to the poorer, communal circumstances of his new life.

Okelo was the first of many children to come to the Kijomanyi Home as a result of brutal killings by Amin's soldiers. In the months that followed the murder of the Okelo family, Amin orphaned thousands of Ugandan children. Soon in every town and village there were dozens of young boys and girls who had witnessed the torturous, bestial deaths of their parents. As I traveled throughout southern Uganda collecting children for the home, I heard many terrifying stories. And I became convinced that the regime of Idi Amin was not merely tyrannical but demonic.*

Here's the amazing part of the story. Under that kind of persecution, Pastor Sempangi's church grew to 14,000 members! Fourteen thousand people stood nose to nose with Idi Amin, squared their shoulders and said, "You can rape our mothers, kill our fathers, and torture our children, Mr. Amin. But we will not compromise. We will not sell out. We have no price." Where in America can we find conviction like that? I sincerely hope that we can find it in your family, and in mine.

Thank God for Pastor Sempangi and the dear people in his church, people of whom the world is not worthy (Heb. 11:38). Because of their examples, I can look my son in the eyes and say, "Yes, David, I know of some people who refuse to compromise their beliefs. And that's what I want you to be like when you grow up."

A person can easily recover from the chicken pox. It's quite another thing to recover from the subtle sellout of one's own soul.

---

*F. Kefa Sempangi, *A Distant Grief* (Ventura: Regal Books, 1979), pp. 47-49.